ASHE Higher Education Report: Volume 31, Number 3
Kelly Ward, Lisa E. Wolf-Wendel, Series Editors

Liberal Arts Colleges and Liberal Arts Education

New Evidence on Impacts

Ernest T. Pascarella, Gregory C. Wolniak,
Tricia A. D. Seifert, Ty M. Cruce, and
Charles F. Blaich

Liberal Arts Colleges and Liberal Arts Education: New Evidence on Impacts
Ernest T. Pascarella, Gregory C. Wolniak, Tricia A. D. Seifert, Ty M. Cruce,
Charles F. Blaich
ASHE Higher Education Report: Volume 31, Number 3
Kelly Ward, Lisa Wolf-Wendel, Series Editors

ISSN 1551-6970   electronic ISSN 1554-6306   ISBN 0-7879-8123-0

The ASHE Higher Education Report is part of the Jossey-Bass Higher and Adult
Education Series and is published six times a year by Wiley Subscription Services,
Inc., A Wiley Company, at Jossey-Bass, 989 Market Street, San Francisco,
California 94103-1741.

For subscription information, see the Back Issue/Subscription Order Form
in the back of this volume.

CALL FOR PROPOSALS: Prospective authors are strongly encouraged to contact
Kelly Ward (kaward@wsu.edu) or Lisa Wolf-Wendel (lwolf@ku.edu). See "About
the ASHE Higher Education Report Series" in the back of this volume.

Visit the Jossey-Bass Web site at **www.josseybass.com.**

Printed in the United States of America on acid-free recycled paper.

Advisory Board

The ASHE Higher Education Report Series is sponsored by the Association for the Study of Higher Education (ASHE), which provides an editorial advisory board of ASHE members.

Contents

Executive Summary

Since its inception (with the founding of Harvard in 1632), the American postsecondary education enterprise has placed great faith in liberal arts colleges and liberal arts education to provide an influential and transforming undergraduate experience. Although much has been written extolling the virtues and benefits of a liberal arts education, relatively little systematic inquiry has estimated its unique effects on student development during college and alumni lives subsequent to graduation. This study summarizes the findings of a multi-institutional study of the short- and long-term effects of liberal arts colleges and liberal arts education using two longitudinal datasets that together contain information about more than 6,500 students and alumni from more than forty institutions throughout the country. The longitudinal nature of both datasets allowed us to conduct analyses in a way that avoids a major methodological problem in much of the existing research. Specifically, we were able to estimate the net effects of liberal arts colleges while controlling for many potentially biasing influences of students' precollege characteristics—including in many instances parallel precollege scores on outcome measures.

The study sought answers to the following questions:

1. To what extent do liberal arts colleges uniquely foster empirically validated good practices in undergraduate education?
2. What are the unique or net impacts of liberal arts colleges, an institution's liberal arts emphasis, and students' liberal arts experiences on intellectual and personal growth during college?

3. What are the net long-term impacts of attending a liberal arts college on the professional and personal lives of alumni?
4. Are the impacts of liberal arts colleges, an institution's liberal arts emphasis, and students' liberal arts experiences the same for all students, or do they differ in magnitude for different kinds of students?

Major Findings: Good Practices

With statistical controls for important confounding influences, evidence was consistent that, compared with research universities and regional institutions, liberal arts colleges do, in fact, uniquely foster a wide range of empirically vetted good practices in undergraduate education. On some good practices, such as extracurricular involvement and other measures of influential interaction with student peers, the positive influence of liberal arts colleges was attributable to their residential full-time student body. On a broad range of other good practices, however, the positive effects of liberal arts colleges were not attributable to those institutions' residential full-time character, academic selectivity, or the precollege characteristics of the students enrolled. These good practice dimensions included student-faculty contact, active learning and time on task, high expectations, quality of teaching, and a supportive campus environment.

Major Findings: Intellectual and Personal Development

Although it is clear that liberal arts colleges fostered the conditions that tend to produce an influential undergraduate experience, the estimated net impacts of attendance at a liberal arts college on measures of intellectual and personal development were mixed. Of eleven different measures of intellectual and personal growth considered in the investigation, liberal arts colleges had no significant influence on two measures (plans to obtain a graduate degree and internal locus of attribution for academic success), negative effects on two measures (mathematics and science reasoning), and mixed effects on two measures (positive attitude toward literacy and preference for higher-order cognitive tasks). Liberal arts colleges in the aggregate demonstrated a positive net impact on openness to diversity and challenge, learning for self-understanding, and writing skills, while selective liberal arts colleges positively influenced not only those outcomes but also growth in reading comprehension and critical thinking. Interestingly, the impact of selective liberal arts colleges on measures of intellectual and personal growth was not shaped in a major way by the academic selectivity of their students. Whether or not we controlled for a measure of the average academic ability of an institution's students altered the estimated effects of selective liberal arts colleges in only inconsistent and minor ways.

We hypothesize that one reason for the mixed effects of liberal arts colleges on students' intellectual and personal development is that institutional type (liberal arts colleges, research universities, regional institutions) may be a structural characteristic that is too general and remote to adequately capture the full impact of liberal arts education. What may count more in the explanation of students' intellectual and personal growth are environmental characteristics and individual experiences that provide a more proximal and construct-valid expression of a liberal arts education than simply attending a liberal arts college. To test the validity of this "hypothesis," we used the theoretical and empirical literature to construct several psychometrically reliable scales operationalizing salient components of a liberal arts education or experience (for example, extensive interaction between students and faculty, faculty emphasis on effective teaching, academic challenge and high expectations, an integrated intellectual experience, extensive student extracurricular involvement and interaction with peers, emphasis on a residential experience). These measures were two aggregate-level indicators of an institution's "liberal arts emphasis" and an individual-level measure of students' "liberal arts experiences." Net of student background characteristics, all three measures were strongly predicted by attendance at a liberal arts college—evidence of their construct validity. These measures of an institution's liberal arts emphasis and students' liberal arts experiences, however, were generally more consistent and positive net predictors of students' intellectual growth in college than was institutional type. Moreover, these estimated effects persisted in the presence of statistical controls not only for students' precollege characteristics but also for institutional selectivity and institutional type. This outcome suggests that, although a liberal arts emphasis and liberal arts experiences are most likely at liberal arts colleges, they are not exclusive to those institutions. When implemented and nurtured at research universities and regional institutions, they have important impacts on students' intellectual and personal growth.

Major Findings: Long-Term Effects

Our analyses of the long-term effects of liberal arts colleges followed samples of alumni from private baccalaureate-level liberal arts colleges, public regional universities, and private master's level institutions located in four different states in the Appalachian region for five, fifteen, and twenty-five years after graduation from college. Statistically controlling for an extensive set of precollege characteristics and other confounding influences, the most consistent differences were between baccalaureate liberal arts colleges and public regional universities. Compared with demographically similar graduates of public regional universities, liberal arts college alumni were not only more satisfied with their undergraduate education but also reported that their undergraduate experience had a significantly stronger impact on their learning and intellectual development, development of leadership and self-efficacy skills, personal and spiritual development, and development of responsible citizenship. Similarly, compared with public regional university alumni, baccalaureate liberal arts college graduates had higher levels of graduate degree attainment; were more likely to be employed in a nonprofit organization and to report that their undergraduate experience prepared them for their first and current jobs; reported a higher level of religious involvement and donated a larger percentage of income to charity; took more continuing education courses for personal development and had a lower level of alcohol consumption; were more likely to be working in the Appalachian region; and were more likely to report that learning and intellectual development, personal and spiritual growth, and responsible citizenship were important in their current lives. Liberal arts college alumni were less likely to be employed full time, had lower annual salaries, were less likely to vote in national elections, and were less likely to campaign for a political candidate.

Major Findings: Conditional Effects

We found little to indicate that the effects of attending a liberal arts college on good practices and measures of intellectual and personal development differed in magnitude for different kinds of students. That is, the estimated effects tended to be equal in magnitude for men and women, for white students and students of color, for students of different ages and with different levels of precollege tested academic ability, and for students who entered college with different precollege scores on each measure of intellectual and personal development considered.

In contrast with the estimated impact of attending a liberal arts college, evidence consistently indicated that the effects on intellectual and personal growth of both an institution's liberal arts emphasis and students' liberal arts experiences were conditional rather than general. Specifically, the effects varied in magnitude based on differences in precollege scores on the measures of intellectual and personal development considered in the study, race, and sex. The clear weight of evidence indicated that an institution's liberal arts emphasis and students' liberal arts experiences may function in a compensatory manner. That is, an institution's liberal arts emphasis and students' liberal arts experiences tended to have stronger positive effects on intellectual and personal growth for students who began college relatively low on these dimensions than for their counterparts who started postsecondary education with relatively high levels of intellectual and personal development. Though less extensive, evidence also suggested that the cognitive benefits of an institution's liberal arts emphasis and students' liberal arts experiences accrued more to students of color than to their white peers and to women more than to men.

Foreword

Liberal arts colleges typify what practitioners and scholars think of as the collegiate ideal: a relatively intimate family-like campus culture, full-time residential students, faculty who are committed to working collaboratively with their students both inside and outside the classroom, and a strong emphasis on fostering students' involvement in both academic and social activities. In this monograph, the authors use empirical data to demonstrate that the collegiate ideal of liberal arts colleges is not imagined but is, indeed, a fact. This monograph shows clearly that liberal arts colleges are more likely than other institutional types to engage in practices and policies associated with the collegiate ideal.

Although the ASHE monograph series does not typically publish original studies, we believe the data offered in this study make such an important contribution to the literature that we decided to try something different. The findings in this monograph are particularly important because they come at a time when liberal arts colleges are rapidly disappearing. The number of liberal arts colleges is declining because many are becoming comprehensive colleges by adding professional master's degrees. The results of the study presented in this monograph suggest that liberal arts colleges are an institutional type worth saving.

Interestingly, however, this monograph concludes that despite the fact that liberal arts colleges are more likely than other institutional types to follow accepted good practices in undergraduate education, these institutions have not cornered the market on positive outcomes for students. Indeed, other institutional types demonstrate positive outcomes as well. This finding lends credence to the conclusion drawn by Pascarella and Terenzini (1991) that when studies control for the characteristics that students bring with them to college, institutional characteristics (such as size, selectivity, and control) have very little effect on student outcomes. In other words, it does not really matter where you go to college: positive outcomes are achieved by students attending all types of institutions. The present study adds an interesting wrinkle to this earlier conclusion by finding that institutions (regardless of type) that offer the characteristics of liberal arts colleges yielded higher scores on intellectual and personal development measures. This monograph provides evidence to support the idea that it is worthwhile for other institutional types to imitate the traits of liberal arts colleges to help their students achieve desired educational outcomes. It also provides further research-based support for the idea that the best practices in undergraduate education are indeed best practices.

This monograph makes an important and significant contribution to the field by demonstrating that liberal arts colleges and the traits associated with them ought to be emulated and preserved. The monograph uses sound longitudinal data from a representative sample of institutions, using measures that are both reliable and valid, to make its case. This study also explores outcomes associated with graduating from different institutional types, though the sample for this part of the study is limited by its geographical emphasis on the Appalachian region.

The contributions made by this monograph to the literature are important for many reasons. In particular, the importance of this monograph is that its conclusions about liberal arts education comes at a time when so many institutions that have their roots in the liberal arts are being forced by market pressures to move toward more comprehensive missions. These same institutions are hiring more adjunct and part-time faculty and are therefore less likely to be able to offer their students what has been demonstrated to be the best practices in undergraduate education. Although studies like this one are not likely to stop institutions buffeted by market forces from changing their focus and missions, it should give them pause to maintain those elements we know serve students best.

Lisa E. Wolf-Wendel
Series Editor

Acknowledgments

The research on which this report was based was sponsored by the Center of Inquiry in the Liberal Arts at Wabash College. We are also indebted to the Mellon and Spencer Foundations and the U.S. Department of Education for supporting collection of the data analyzed in the report.

Background and Warrant
for the Study

THE LIBERAL ARTS COLLEGE is the oldest form of higher education in the United States. With the founding of Harvard in 1636, the United States set forth what would become a tradition of education deemed "distinctively American" (Koblik and Graubard, 2000). According to Koblik (2000), residential liberal arts colleges in the United States stand alone in their total dedication to undergraduate education. An abundance of virtues have been connected to this form of higher education. Hill (1994) attributed the development of magnanimity and justice to liberal arts education. Spaeth (1986) and Cronon (1999) credited the liberal arts with the development of truth and humility, while Rosenfield (1985) ascribed active citizenship as a result of liberal arts education. Although much has been written extolling the virtues and benefits of a liberal arts education, relatively few empirical efforts have attempted to identify its unique effects on student development (Center of Inquiry in the Liberal Arts, 2004). The few studies that have been conducted have focused on different and narrow aspects of liberal arts colleges. As such, the resulting body of knowledge about the impacts of liberal arts colleges on students lacks any genuine systematic integration.

This report attempts to contribute to our understanding of liberal arts colleges and liberal arts education by synthesizing the results of four sets of analyses. First, we examined whether differences existed in how students at liberal arts colleges, in comparison with their peers at research universities or public regional institutions, experience "good practices in undergraduate education" (Chickering and Gamson, 1987, 1991). Second, we investigated whether liberal arts colleges uniquely impact students' intellectual and personal development during college. Our third set of analyses was guided by the notion that an institution's ethos may have an influential impact on students. Moving beyond the more traditional institutional type comparison, we synthesized pedagogical practices and experiences associated with liberal arts education by creating a scale we consider to capture an institution's *liberal arts emphasis* and investigated how a *liberal arts emphasis* influenced student development during college. Fourth, we investigated the long-term effects of attending a baccalaureate liberal arts college (versus a public regional or a private master's level institution) on graduates' work and life experiences. In each set of analyses, we additionally explored whether differences in the estimated effects of liberal arts colleges occur in magnitude for different kinds of students (for example, differences in race, sex, precollege educational characteristics, and the like). Together, our analyses form a comprehensive effort to systematically study liberal arts colleges and liberal arts education by assessing the impacts of different institutional types and different institutional ethos on students both during college and beyond.

Review of Existing Evidence

The literature on liberal arts colleges and, more generally, on liberal arts education spans many decades and disciplines. In his philosophical treatise, John Henry Cardinal Newman (1853/1996) described the purpose of a liberal arts education as well as the benefits individuals realized from it. Others have situated liberal arts colleges and liberal arts education of the United States in historical, social, and political contexts (Breneman, 1990, 1994b; Durden, 2002; Hawkins, 2000; Hersh, 1997; Marshall, 2003; McPherson, 1998; Rudolph, 1990). Educational researchers have also considered liberal arts colleges and liberal arts education from the perspective of a pedagogical experience, investigating their effects on intellectual and personal development (Hayek and Kuh, 1998; Kuh and Hu, 2001; Pace, 1997; Pace and Connolly, 2000; Umbach and Kuh, forthcoming; Winter, McClelland, and Stewart, 1981).

With volumes of books and complete journals dedicated to discussing the ideas and values of "liberal education," this review cannot begin to be exhaustive. Yet we seek to provide a meaningful context for a discussion of the impacts of liberal arts colleges and liberal arts education. The review of the existing evidence is framed in two sections. The initial section describes the nonempirical literature by situating liberal arts colleges in a historical context, contrasting the historical liberal arts college model with the present. We follow by detailing the vast heterogeneity within the institutional category commonly considered "liberal arts colleges, and we conclude by characterizing the modern challenges faced by liberal arts colleges and liberal arts education. The subsequent section reviews the empirical literature, focusing on what is known about the unique effects of attending a liberal arts college on students' engagement in the postsecondary experience, their intellectual and personal development, and their career success and personal lives after college.

Liberal Arts Colleges: Past and Present

Higher education in the United States is rooted in the liberal arts college (Rudolph, 1990). Modeled after Oxford and Cambridge in England, the American liberal arts college was small and residential, with traditional-age full-time male students studying a common curriculum, culminating in a bachelor's degree. The college was typically situated in a bucolic environment apart from the vice of the city in an effort to focus students' attention on their intellectual pursuits (Rudolph, 1990).

The historic purpose of the liberal arts college was to educate young men in a manner befitting civic and religious leaders of the Colonies. Calling on the tradition of the ancient Greeks, a liberal arts education[1] was intended to free students from the bondage of habit and custom by tempering profound parochial convictions with a measure of tolerance and a judicious sense of humility (Freedman, 2000; Nussbaum, 1997). Moreover, a liberal arts education focused on the development of the "whole person" (Conrad and Wyer, 1982; Hawkins, 2000; Lang, 2000) by teaching students to understand not only themselves but also the foundations of a democratic society and the responsibilities of citizenship. This noble task was accomplished by introducing students to the methods of reasoning and instilling in them an understanding of the proper balance between the opportunities for individualism and the demands of community (Freedman, 2000).

Today's liberal arts colleges vary greatly from the historic image. Although many liberal arts colleges remain small and residential, most are coeducational and can be found in cities as well as small towns. Some are highly selective and boast large endowments while others have a virtually open admission policy and are heavily tuition dependent (Astin, 2000; Koblik, 2000). Variations between liberal arts colleges also include the level of religious affiliation, proportion of degrees granted to students in traditional liberal arts disciplines, and the financial base of the institution (Astin and Lee, 1972; Breneman, 1990, 1994b; Carnegie Foundation for the Advancement of Teaching, 2000; Pace, 1974). Despite this heterogeneity, the overwhelming mission of the educational experience remains to liberally educate the whole person (Breneman, 1990).

Typologies of Liberal Arts Colleges

Many of today's liberal arts colleges boast of the historical purpose and benefits of a liberal arts education to their students and stakeholders (Aleman and Salkever, 2002). In today's diverse environment of higher education institutions, however, the simple act of identifying and defining liberal arts colleges is a complex and at times contentious practice. In an attempt to differentiate between institutional types in American higher education, Pace (1974) employed a cluster analysis of the College and University Environment Scales (CUES) to distinguish eight distinct institutional types, three of which were variations of the liberal arts college (Pace, 1974). These efforts distinguished between the selective liberal arts college, the denominational liberal arts college, and the general liberal arts college, based on the characteristics of institutional intellectual emphasis and degree of religious affiliation. For example, the selective liberal arts college was defined as academically selective, private, nonsectarian, and intellectually demanding; the denominational liberal arts college was strongly denominational, either Catholic or Protestant; and the general liberal arts colleges comprised some denominational and some nonsectarian colleges, but not as strongly denominational as the denominational liberal arts colleges or as highly selective or intellectually demanding as the selective liberal arts colleges.

Similar to the typology defined by the College and University Environment Scales, the Carnegie classification created by the Carnegie Foundation for the Advancement of Teaching has also used the selective nature of liberal arts colleges to draw institutional distinctions. In 1973, the classification separated liberal arts colleges into two groups. The differentiation rested on the selectivity of admissions and the number of graduates who went on to complete the Ph.D. at "leading" universities (Carnegie Foundation for the Advancement of Teaching, 2000). The latter criterion was removed from the classification scheme in 1987 and was replaced with a measure of the percentage of degrees awarded in traditional liberal arts disciplines. In 1994, categories such as Baccalaureate (Liberal Arts) Colleges I and Baccalaureate Colleges II were created based on whether 40 percent of degrees awarded were in a liberal arts discipline as well as the selectivity of the institution. More recently, the 2000 Carnegie classification eliminated selectivity as a distinguishing characteristic and raised the threshold of degrees granted in liberal arts disciplines to 50 percent, resulting in a category distinguishing between Baccalaureate Colleges–Liberal Arts and Baccalaureate Colleges–General (Carnegie Foundation for the Advancement of Teaching, 2000). Under the 2000 Carnegie criteria, 228 colleges remain with the distinction of Baccalaureate Colleges–Liberal Arts.

Before Carnegie's use of the percentage of degrees awarded in traditional liberal arts disciplines as a distinguishing criterion, Breneman (1990, 1994b) used percentage of degrees awarded in liberal arts disciplines and the source of institutional revenue as the criteria for another typology of liberal arts colleges. Based on these two criteria, liberal arts colleges were divided into two halves: those colleges that granted 40 percent or more of their degrees in liberal arts disciplines and were financially rooted in revenue from undergraduate programs; and those colleges that granted fewer than 40 percent of their degrees to students in liberal arts disciplines and had a financial base that included professional and graduate programs. The latter Breneman labeled "small professional colleges." Under these criteria, the number of liberal arts colleges in the United States decreased to 212.

Although the number of traditional liberal arts colleges has decreased, Breneman (1990, 1994b) concluded that, despite the decline in total numbers, liberal arts colleges were not failing but rather evolving to meet the needs of a changing economy. Alternatively, Delucchi (1997) criticized the curricular shifts taking place at many liberal arts colleges, particularly those Breneman classified as small professional colleges, arguing that there is a "liberal arts myth" in institutions' efforts to legitimately connect themselves to their more selective and high status peer institutions. Ultimately, the classification system used to distinguish between institution types and the debates over identifying and defining liberal arts colleges is one of the dynamic characteristics of American higher education.

Challenges to Liberal Arts Colleges and Liberal Arts Education

Liberal arts colleges have faced and continue to face a host of challenges. Their existence has been threatened by the increased focus of postsecondary education on vocational education.[2] Additionally, liberal arts colleges are confronted by the public's lack of understanding of or complete misperception about the goals and benefits of liberal arts education and career skills. Finally, the public disconnect between the goals and benefits of liberal arts education and career skills leads to a belief that a liberal arts education and attending a liberal arts college are luxury educational experiences for the wealthy. This section discusses the challenges faced by liberal arts colleges and liberal arts education in greater detail.

Historically, one of the greatest challenges to the liberal arts has come from vocational education (Brint, 2002; Freedman, 2000; MacTaggart, 1993; Miles, 1986; Neely, 2000; Rudolph, 1990; Scott, 1992; Shea, 1993; Thelin, 2004). Curricular changes have been a common feature in American higher education and have been the most direct manifestation of the tension in defining and meeting the evolving public and private need (Grubb and Lazerson, 2005; Lattuca and Stark, 2001; Rudolph, 1990; Thelin 2004). During the last two centuries, high schools, colleges, universities, and (more recently) community colleges have at different times responded to the often conflicting demands of a democratic and capitalistic society (Labaree, 1990). In a changing economic and political context, students and their families have sought higher education that would fulfill their aspirations for economic success and social mobility. At times, these goals have been best served by a liberal arts education, while at others and for many of the same reasons, students and their families have found vocationally oriented education to best serve their goals. Thus, the value placed on liberal arts education by the populace has largely been a function of the economic and political context of the society.

During the colonial period, a liberal arts education was seen as cultivating broad rather than specialized skills and was thus viewed as imminently useful for serving the needs of the Colonies. By the early 1800s, however, not all members of the citizenry embraced these same broad skills resulting from a liberal arts education. Critics of liberal arts education found the curriculum provided inadequately for the emerging needs of society. Yet these first cries for a "new modeled" (Rudolph, 1990, p. 132) curricula were met with sharp criticism. The Yale Report (Goodchild and Wechsler, 1828/1997), a bold statement defending the traditional curricula, repeatedly stressed the purpose of a college education was to build a foundation that serves the vast and ever-changing needs of society. The report concluded that the business character of the nation was best served through the traditional liberal arts curriculum.

As the Industrial Revolution flourished at the end of the nineteenth century, the traditional liberal arts curriculum was threatened by the notion that colleges "should train citizens to participate in the nation's economic and commercial life . . . through the offering of career-oriented programs buttressed by general education electives" (Lattuca and Stark, 2001, p. 4). Rudolph (1990) characterized developments in higher education in the years following the Civil War as a "redefinition" (p. 241), where "everywhere the idea of going to college was being liberated from the class-bound, classical-bound traditions which for so long had defined the American college experience" (p. 263). With the growing industrial economy and the rise of the professions, students recognized the value given to school-based knowledge over work-based knowledge and obtained this professional expertise from universities that could provide the necessary credentials (Grubb and Lazerson, 2005). In contrast, the dismal job markets of the Great Depression fueled students' desire to major in traditional liberal arts disciplines to acquire the broad skills that provided career flexibility (Lattuca and Stark, 2001).

More than any previous time period, the American higher education expansion of the 1940s, 1950s, and 1960s impacted the role of liberal arts education. Represented in the 1947 *Report of the President's Commission on*

Higher Education (Goodchild and Wechsler, 1989), higher education was intended to educate *all* citizens for the purpose of creating a better nation and a better world. The vocationally oriented curriculum provided many first-generation college students, pursuing postsecondary education through the G.I. bill, career opportunities and social mobility. This more career-focused curriculum was fervently embraced during the dim economic climate of the 1970s. In marked contrast to the Great Depression, students of this era chose to pursue majors with a more direct link to occupations (College Placement Council, 1975). Brint (2002) starkly describes this shift away from traditional liberal arts majors: "During a period in which the system grew by 50 percent [1970–71 to 2000–01], almost every field which constituted the old arts and sciences core of the undergraduate college was in absolute decline. This includes not only all of the humanities and social sciences (except psychology and economics) but also the physical sciences and mathematics" (p. 235). Gauging from student choice, a liberal arts education was not perceived as preparing students with occupational skills (Bonvillian and Murphy, 1996; Winter, McClelland, and Stewart, 1981).

With a debatable amount of success, many higher education institutions have used some form of general education program as the primary means of accomplishing the attributes[3] associated with the formal curriculum of a liberal arts college (Rudolph, 1990). Through the last three decades, the tension between liberal arts and vocationally oriented education has changed form. Rather than the previous either/or approach, many supporters of postsecondary education have called for a uniting synthesis of both a liberal arts education with a vocational focus and a vocationally oriented curriculum grounded in liberal learning (Chickering, 1982; Durden, 2003; Gorelick, 1982; Green and Salem, 1988; Schwerin, 1983; Stark, 1987). Although it is unclear how this synthesizing approach may substantively differ from general education, it appears to move the previous tension into a direction of mutual reinforcement, a potential boon for both liberal arts and vocationally oriented education.

Although the higher education community has recognized the need for a synthesis of liberal arts and vocationally oriented education, economic considerations remain prominent in the minds of prospective college students and their families. The parents of today's traditional-age college students were of traditional college age during the 1970s and often carry the perception that a liberal arts education does not provide marketable career skills. Reviewing public opinion surveys of more than 1,200 people, including community leaders, Immerwahr and Harvey (1995) found 79 percent of respondents equated college with better jobs but were unclear as to the specific goals of higher education and particularly liberal arts education. Although the goals of liberal arts education were a mystery to many respondents, community leaders joined the higher education community in recognizing a need for a synthesized curriculum, citing the importance of gaining the broad contextual understanding provided by the liberal arts with proficiency in technical and professional skills.

Hersh (1997) reported a similar lack of understanding regarding the goals of a liberal arts education. Hersh's study surveyed five stakeholder groups as to their feelings regarding important aspects of higher education and familiarity with liberal arts education. Each group (college-bound juniors and seniors, parents of college-bound students, CEOs and human resource managers, university and liberal arts college graduates, and high school and college faculty and administrators) reported that developing career skills was the most important aspect of higher education. These stakeholders also rated problem solving, critical thinking, written and oral skills, strong work habits, self-discipline, and a respect for others as the most important goals of higher education (Hersh, 1997). It is logical to conclude then that the identified goals of higher education (problem solving, critical thinking, written and oral skills) should buttress the key aspect of higher education (development of career skills).

Interestingly, liberal arts educators have long embraced these goals as central to the mission of a liberal arts education (American Association for Liberal Education, 2004; Association of American Colleges and Universities, 1998; Schneider and Shoenberg, 1998). Yet Hersh (1997) found 44 percent of college-bound high school students and 27 percent of their parents responded that they were unfamiliar with liberal arts education. This finding suggests that students and parents tend to be unaware of the connection between the goals of a liberal arts education and career skills. Barker (2000) stated in the Carnegie Commission report, *Liberal Arts Education for a Global Society*, that liberal arts educators must recognize that the benefits of a liberal arts education are not self-evident. Likewise, the claim "learning for the sake of learning" is not particularly salient for consumers who are concerned with the increased debt burden of college and focused on the degree to which a liberal arts education contributes to career opportunities (Barker, 2000).

Premising his study on the belief that little is known about conceptions and perceptions of contemporary liberal arts education beyond historical overview, philosophical analysis, or rhetorical persuasion, Atkinson (1997) reported current college students as well as faculty and other stakeholders lacked clarity in understanding the basic concepts of liberal arts education. These findings suggest students are left on their own to draw connections between the skills developed by a liberal arts education and the career skills sought by employers. Based on Atkinson's results, it appears students have not readily made this connection. Seventy-five percent of seniors, faculty, and administrators in the sample agreed with the statement "students believe liberal [arts] education will not help in getting a job" (Atkinson, Swanson, and Reardon, 1998, p. 26).

The widespread misperceptions about liberal arts education provide a significant challenge for its advocates. During the 1990s, college freshmen considered the ability to make more money and get a better job the most important reasons in their decision to enter college (Astin, 1993). Coupled with long-term trends of increasing direct costs of attending four-year institutions (Heller, 2001; Kane, 1999; Paulsen and Smart, 2001), students' decisions for an education that accompanies labor market rewards make them acutely aware of the relationship between their college education, resulting skills, and job opportunities. Considering that tuition is increasing at an alarming rate (Boehner and McKeon, 2003), one can assume the concern regarding return on educational investment will only continue at the current pace. To a great extent, the future of liberal arts education depends on its supporters' ability to cogently articulate the connection between the skills developed (for example, problem solving, critical thinking, oral and written communication, respect for different points of view) and the skills valued by employers.

Even if the advocates of liberal arts education changed public perception, successfully articulating the connection between the goals of liberal arts education and career skills, many people believe a liberal arts education is affordable only for the wealthy (Breneman, 1994a; Durden, 2002; Freedman, 2000; Hersh, 1997). Hersh found six out of ten parents and more than 50 percent of high school students in the sample viewed higher education, in general, as too expensive. But an additional 19 percent of parents and 24 percent of students, along with more than 30 percent of respondents in the other stakeholder categories, believed the issue of "too expensive" was true only for attending a liberal arts college. Astin (2000) reported that the public equates a residential liberal arts education with an elite and largely inaccessible form of higher education. Carnevale and Strohl (2001) stated the future of liberal arts education is unclear, given the popular bias that views liberal arts education to be too expensive for the mass of U.S. students. Moreover, one-third of parents agreed with the statement "a liberal arts education is a luxury most people cannot afford" (Hersh, 1997, p. 22).

Liberal arts colleges, in particular, are threatened by the perception that liberal arts education is a luxury. The liberal arts college is a small niche within the modern American higher education landscape (Neely, 2000). Because of their size, liberal arts colleges are not able to capitalize on economies of scale (Bonvillian and Murphy, 1996). Additionally, the mission of most liberal arts colleges to develop the "whole person," typically accompanied by greater student service expenditures (McPherson and Shapiro, 2000) and a smaller student-to-faculty ratio than other institutional types, tends to increase financial expenditures. Moreover, the common practice of tuition discounting requires institutions to focus on the difficult challenge of predicting net tuition revenue in their forecasting or face an erosion of critical resources (Hubbell and Rush, 1991). These challenges, coupled with the volatility of endowment earnings (Pratt, 2003), can work against the financial viability of liberal arts colleges and may lead to greater vulnerability to the competition from lower-priced public institutions.

Liberal arts colleges, although descending from a common historical mission, vary greatly (Astin and Lee, 1972; Breneman, 1990, 1994b; Pace, 1974). The vast heterogeneity of the institutions known as "liberal arts colleges" particularly limits the ability to empirically draw generalizations about their impact (Astin and Lee, 1972). Thus, the imperative for the supporters of liberal arts education is to, as Mohrman (1999) exhorts, "know what a liberal arts education represents" (p. 9) and to widely communicate its value in developing students who have a "strong sense of self and habits of the mind and action to become leaders" (Durden, 2002, p. 26).

Evidence About the Impacts of Liberal Arts Colleges

To date, many of the claims made by the proponents of liberal arts education have not been empirically substantiated. Some of those who are the most invested in liberal arts education, particularly at selective liberal arts colleges, believe the benefits of a liberal arts education are self-evident and do not need to be empirically justified (Atkinson, 1997; Winter, McClelland, and Stewart, 1981). Even when the benefits are assessed, the "guardians" of liberal education favor rhetoric and personal testimony (Bird, 1975; Wilkinson, 1964) over quantitative methods. Many have argued that the benefits of a liberal arts education defy quantification (Winter, McClelland, and Stewart, 1981).

In their review and synthesis of past research, Pascarella and Terenzini (1991) noted that relatively few sizable differences existed in the unique or net impacts of different types of institutions. Rather, they asserted the importance of a "supportive social-psychological context" (p. 596) in contributing to institutional impact. Such a context includes items like a strong faculty emphasis on teaching and student development, a common valuing of the life of the mind, small size, a shared intellectual experience, high academic expectations, and frequent interactions inside and outside the classroom between students and faculty (Pascarella and Terenzini, 1998). Although these environmental traits tend to appear most often at small, private liberal arts colleges, and particularly selective liberal arts colleges, it is the manifested environment of an institution rather than a specific institutional type that impacts student intellectual and personal development (Pascarella and Terenzini, 1991).

The empirical research investigating the unique or net impact of attending a liberal arts college (relative to other types of institutions) on students' intellectual and personal development is not comprehensive (Center of Inquiry in the Liberal Arts, 2004). Rather, the research tends to be divisive, unsystematic, lacking coherent organization, and varying widely in the comparisons made.

For example, several studies have investigated changes in student intellectual and personal development at a single liberal arts college (Frieden Graham, 1989; Heath, 1968, 1976; Stratton, 1990). Although these studies contribute to our overall understanding, they do not allow for a comparison of the unique impacts of attending a liberal arts college versus other types of institutions. Other studies have compared the unique effects of liberal arts colleges to either research universities or public regional/comprehensive institutions. Additionally, as a result of the great degree of heterogeneity in liberal arts colleges, a number of studies have also estimated the unique effects that different types of liberal arts colleges (for example, selective liberal arts colleges versus general liberal arts colleges or vocational liberal arts colleges) have on student development.

Together, this body of research provides an empirical base from which we can begin to understand the impacts of attending a liberal arts college on a host of students' intellectual and developmental outcomes. In an effort to simplify our review of the empirical evidence, we focus on studies comparing liberal arts colleges with other types of institutions in terms of students' engagement in educational activities, intellectual and personal development, and educational persistence, and long-term effects of liberal arts colleges.

Engagement in Educational Activities

Pascarella and Terenzini (1991) asserted that a "supportive social-psychological context" (p. 596) tends to be the hallmark trait most frequently found in small liberal arts colleges. Astin (2000) uncovered evidence of such an environment at the small liberal arts colleges in his review of data through the 1990s as well as a national longitudinal study of 135 private liberal arts colleges comparing selective liberal arts colleges, liberal arts colleges, and other types of institutions (Astin, 1993; Pascarella and Terenzini, 1991). Students at liberal arts colleges, regardless of selectivity, reported greater satisfaction with the faculty, quality of teaching, and general education program than their peers at other institutional types. Controlling for student background characteristics, students at liberal arts colleges also reported having greater trust in the administration and viewed the institution as more student oriented and more focused on social change (Astin, 2000).

Given that liberal arts colleges tend to be characterized by socially and psychologically supportive environments, one might conclude students at liberal arts colleges are more engaged in educational activities. We found, however, that the evidence suggests a more complex relationship between institutional type and levels of engagement in educationally purposeful activities. Pace and Connolly (2000) examined the effect of institutional type on students' engagement in out-of-class conversations. Comparing a cohort of students who completed the College Student Experiences Questionnaire (CSEQ) between 1983 and 1986 with a cohort completing it between 1997 and 1998, Pace and Connolly (2000) found students in the 1980s cohort at selective liberal arts colleges engaged in serious conversations with people different from themselves far more frequently than their peers at research universities. Students at research universities in the 1990s cohort narrowed this gap, however, and in some instances surpassed the level of engagement of their selective liberal arts college peers.

This finding may be the manifestation of more students at research universities engaging in educationally purposeful activities than in selective liberal arts college students' disengagement. Public universities, including research universities, were heavily criticized in the early 1990s for the decline in the quality of undergraduate education (see, for example, National Association of State Universities and Land-Grant Colleges, 1997; Wingspread Group on Higher Education, 1993). Many universities responded with a reinvestment in undergraduate education by creating first-year experiences (see, for example, Upcraft, Gardner, and Associates, 1989) and service-learning programs (Waterman, 1997; Zlotkowski, 2002) as well as increasing undergraduate student contact with faculty (Finkelstein, Seal, and Schuster, 1998). These changes may explain some of the gains in engagement in educationally purposeful activities by students at research universities.

Kuh and Hu (2001) reported that institutional type (as defined by the 1994 Carnegie classification) had a complex impact on students' learning productivity.[4] Comparing cohorts of students from the 1980s and 1990s from a range of institutional types, Kuh and Hu found that students at selective liberal arts colleges maintained greater learning productivity during both time periods, substantiating Pace's findings (1990) that students at selective liberal arts colleges, versus all other institutions, had significantly higher scores on many quality of effort and involvement scales. Kuh and Hu's results held in the presence of controls for institutional selectivity, students' race and ethnicity, gender, and socioeconomic background. Students at general liberal arts colleges, however, reported decreased participation on six of the seven dimensions associated with learning productivity during the time span studied (Kuh and Hu, 2001).

In a follow-up investigation, Hu and Kuh (2002) found that the magnitude of the change in the learning productivity indicators for general liberal arts colleges was small. Moreover, in comparison with their peers at research universities and comprehensive colleges, students at liberal arts colleges of all levels of selectivity tended to be more engaged. Distinguishing among liberal arts colleges, Hu and Kuh found that students at general liberal arts colleges tended more often to be labeled as engaged (23.2 percent) than their peers at selective liberal arts colleges (15.0 percent). In addition, although using a different institutional classification scheme,[5] Pace (1997) found students at general liberal arts colleges were more engaged than their peers at vocational liberal arts colleges on nearly a third of 138 educationally purposeful activities (such as use of the library, faculty contacts, involvement in the arts, and conversations about significant societal conditions).

The body of evidence suggests that the socially and psychologically supportive campus environment of liberal arts colleges appears to foster higher levels of student engagement in educational activities. Evidence has also suggested that levels of engagement differ by type of liberal arts college and that increased engagement in educationally purposeful activities does not necessarily lead to greater student learning productivity at all types of liberal arts colleges.

Intellectual Development and Learning Gains

One of the earliest studies investigating the unique effects of attending a liberal arts college versus other institutions was conducted by Winter, McClelland, and Stewart (1981). Using a longitudinal design and controlling for important confounding influences, they compared students at one highly selective liberal arts college with students at one comprehensive state institution and one community college on a measure of intellectual flexibility and consistency in handling conflicting arguments on controversial issues. Over the course of their college years, results indicated that students at the selective liberal arts college showed significantly greater gains on this measure than their peers at the two comparison institutions. Although the controls employed (SAT score and socioeconomic background) give greater credibility to the study's findings, it is important to recognize that these findings may be a result of the type of student recruited by selective liberal arts colleges and not a unique institutional effect. This study is also limited in its generalizability in that its sample consisted of only one institution of each type.

Research since the Winter, McClelland, and Stewart study (1981) has been far more inconsistent in suggesting differences between institutional type on measures of students' intellectual development. Although Kuh (1993) found that students at liberal arts colleges reported greater gains in cognitive complexity than their counterparts at comprehensive colleges, the study did not control for potentially confounding differences in students' background characteristics. Here again, it is difficult to determine just how much of the difference in cognitive complexity could be attributed to differential recruitment effects rather than to institutional impacts. Interestingly, in a recent analysis of 120 institutions participating in the National Study of Student Engagement, Hu and Kuh (2003b) found that students attending selective liberal arts colleges reported fewer gains in intellectual development. Although this study controlled for students' background characteristics, the findings should be interpreted with caution as students at different institutions may use different baselines when reporting gains (Pascarella, 2001).

Despite methodological limitations, Hu and Kuh's findings (2003b) lend support to Pace and Connolly's cohort comparison (2000) of the 1980s to the 1990s on students' progress in attaining outcomes historically associated with the liberal arts (such as breadth of knowledge, values, effective writing, analysis and logic, and problem solving). Using the CSEQ, Pace and Connolly (2000) found that students at selective liberal arts colleges in the 1990s cohort reported making "quite a bit" or "very much" (p. 58) progress toward attaining liberal arts outcomes at roughly the same rate as their peers in the 1980s cohort. In the 1990s, however, this gap narrowed between students at research universities and their peers at selective liberal arts colleges. For example, in the 1980s cohort, selective liberal arts college students had a 23 percent advantage over students at research universities in terms of making "quite a bit" or "very much" progress relative to "becoming aware of different philosophies, culture, and ways of life" (p. 58). In the 1990s cohort, the gap had narrowed, with selective liberal arts college students having only an 11 percent advantage. With regard to the institutional environment in the 1980s cohort, a 32 percent gap existed between students who ranked their institution at six or seven on a seven-point rating scale regarding the institution's emphasis on being critical, evaluative, and analytical. In the 1990s cohort, the gap narrowed to 15 percent.

Pace (1997) also compared students at general liberal arts colleges with students at vocational liberal arts colleges on the extent to which they felt they had gained or made progress on the aforementioned liberal arts goals. For ten of the goals, the percentage of students at general liberal arts colleges indicating substantial progress toward these goals was 10 percent higher than their peers at vocational liberal arts colleges. The only goal in which vocational liberal arts college students responded as making more substantial progress was in regard to vocational training, but this difference was only 4 percentage points.

In addition to inconsistent findings, some studies investigating the impacts of institutional type on learning gains have found no reliable differences. Smart (1997) found, when controls were made for precollege dispositions to enter different fields of study, institutional type was unrelated to self-reports of learning gains. Additionally, a comprehensive study by Pike, Kuh, and Gonyea (2003) found no differences between institutional type (as defined by Carnegie classification) and students' self-reported learning gains.

Although the evidence strongly suggests the absence of a meaningful link between institutional type and self-reported learning gains, Hayek and Kuh (1998) did find that institutional type may impact lifelong learning. Comparing college seniors' self-evaluation of skills considered important for lifelong learning, Hayek and Kuh investigated students' CSEQ records from the mid-1980s and mid-1990s from a variety of institutional types. They found students at selective liberal arts colleges exhibited the greatest capacity for lifelong learning during both time periods compared with students at general liberal arts colleges, comprehensive colleges, and research universities.

Although areas exist in which attending a liberal arts college does appear to have a unique effect on facets of intellectual development, the weight of the evidence suggests that the impact of institutional type is highly complex and difficult to generalize. Taken as a whole, this body of research suggests that institutional impact on student intellectual development is inconsistent and potentially trivial.

Personal Development

One of the hallmark charges of a liberal arts education is to develop the "whole student" (Conrad and Wyer, 1982; Hawkins, 2000; Lang, 2000) and to develop respect for others (Hersh, 1997; Lagemann, 2003). Previous research that has assessed students in this regard has examined growth in self-definition and the maturity to adapt and personally integrate into the environment (see, for example, Winter, McClelland, and Stewart, 1981), acceptance and appreciation of diverse others (see, for example, Hu and Kuh, 2003a; Umbach and Kuh, forthcoming), and principled moral reasoning (for example, McNeel, 1994).

Winter, McClelland, and Stewart (1981), in their longitudinal study, investigated the effects of a selective liberal arts college on areas of personal development. They focused on measures of, among other things, self-definition (that is, the degree to which one believes his or her actions and efforts produce real effects on the world) and maturity of adaptation and personal integration (that is, the degree to which one develops an integrated and interdependent sense of self with others and authority). Compared with students at the other institutions, students at the selective liberal arts college in the study demonstrated significantly greater gains in both self-definition and the maturity to adapt and integrate with the environment (Winter, McClelland, and Stewart, 1981). These positive impacts of liberal arts colleges on dimensions of maturity found by Winter, McClelland, and Stewart (1981) are consistent with earlier evidence reported by Heath (1968, 1976).

In an ever-increasing multicultural world, respect for others is predicated on respecting the diverse perspectives and experiences of others. Winter, McClelland, and Stewart (1981) found that students experience positive change in their respect for diversity from their freshman to senior years but did not find any distinction in this change between students at different institutions. In other words, respect for diversity appeared to be a general effect of higher education or perhaps simply an artifact of maturing, independent of whether or not a student attended a liberal arts college. Alternatively, Umbach and Kuh (forthcoming) found that despite enrolling proportionately fewer minority students, students at Baccalaureate Colleges–Liberal Arts[6] reported more experiences with diversity than their peers at other types of institutions, when controlling for differences in background characteristics of students and institutional traits (for example, sector, size, urbanicity, and selectivity). Similar findings were reported by Hu and Kuh (2003a), where students at Baccalaureate Colleges–Liberal Arts indicated having more contact and serious discussion with peers from different backgrounds than all other institutional types except Doctoral-Extensive universities, controlling for a host of student and institutional characteristics.

Although it appears that developing respect or appreciation for diversity accompanies the higher education experience in general, diversity-related experiences occur significantly more often at liberal arts colleges. Past research, however, has not been able to assess whether the diversity-related experiences distinctly found at liberal arts colleges have a greater impact on cultivating behavior that respects and appreciates diverse others among students throughout their college years and beyond.

With the "whole student" in mind, liberal arts education has long embraced the goal of developing values and ethics (American Association of State Colleges and Universities, 1976; Brown, 1979; Healy, 1980; O'Brien, 1991). One outcome related to this goal is the development of principled moral reasoning. Using data from a meta-analysis of studies, McNeel (1994) compared students at liberal arts colleges, Bible colleges, and public universities on gains made during college of the Defining Issues Test (a measure of the extent to which one uses principled reasoning in judging moral issues). Results indicated that the largest freshman-to-senior gains in principled moral reasoning were made at the private liberal arts colleges, many of which were religiously affiliated. Relatively smaller but still substantial gains were also made at large, public universities, while the smallest gains were evidenced at the Bible colleges. Good and Cartwright (1998) reported similar findings from a smaller sample of three institutions—one of each type.

McNeel's findings are particularly interesting because respondents in the longitudinal studies from private liberal arts colleges had the highest entering scores on principled reasoning. Yet they experienced the greatest shift from conservative to principled reasoning on moral issues, while the students at the Bible colleges had the lowest entering scores and realized the smallest shift. These two trends are just the opposite of regression artifacts (that is, the artificial tendency for samples that have lower initial scores on a test to show greater gains on the test than samples that start out with initially higher scores on the same test). This finding suggests the real possibility that the between-college differences represent actual institutional effects.

From the perspective of the overall body of evidence, students who attend liberal arts colleges appear to be generally advantaged relative to students at other institutions in measured aspects of personal development (for example, self-definition, engaging in diversity-related experiences, and development of personal moral reasoning). These advantages are perhaps the result of the social and psychologically supportive environment (Astin, 1993, 2000; Pascarella and Terenzini, 1991) or perhaps the result of a historical focus on facilitating the development of the whole student or perhaps the result of the experiences liberal arts colleges appear to distinctly promote involving individuals with diverse backgrounds and views. An important limitation of past research, however, is that we do not know how the kinds of experiences found most often at liberal arts colleges may affect personal development, independent of both student and institutional characteristics.

Educational Persistence and Long-Term Effects

Given the fact of high rates of student dropout (Ishitani and DesJardins, 2002), stopout (Ahson, Gentemann, and Phelps, 1998; Horn, 1998), and institutional transfer (Adelman, 1998; McCormick, 1997), studies investigating the impacts of institutional type on persistence and longer-term outcomes of college face logistical challenges. Nevertheless, several studies have suggested that differences in students' persistence and long-term, postcollege lives are associated with the type of institution attended.

Two studies have investigated students' persistence to the beginning of the second year of college. Results indicated that among public doctoral-degree-granting institutions, persistence rates range from 8 to 15 percentage points greater than at baccalaureate-only institutions, while persistence rates at private doctoral-degree-granting institutions are 8 to 12 percentage points greater than at baccalaureate-only institutions (American College Testing Program, 2002; Consortium for Student Retention Data Exchange, 2002).

In terms of impacts of institutional type on students' employment-related earnings, three studies investigated the economic returns to bachelor's degrees from different Carnegie-classified institutions. Bellas (1998), Monks (2000), and Tsapogas, Cahalan, and Stowe (1994) compared liberal arts colleges with other Carnegie-classified institutions. They found only graduation from specialized institutions (that is, those focusing on professional specialties such as health care, business, and engineering) to consistently lead to significantly greater earnings. Across all three studies, the advantage in average earnings accruing to graduates of specialized institutions was about 19 percent above that of liberal arts college graduates.

Specialized institutions aside, comparisons of the economic returns for a bachelor's degree between liberal arts colleges and other types of institutions have generated inconsistent results (Pascarella and Terenzini, 2005). For example, Tsapogas, Cahalan, and Stowe (1994) used two different datasets to investigate the relationship between institutional type and earnings. Controlling for student background characteristics, work experience, and a measure of institutional selectivity, they found inconclusive results. Although no significant difference in earnings was found between general liberal arts college graduates and their peers at research, doctoral, or comprehensive universities using the National Science Foundation (NSF) New Entrants Survey, the findings from the National Center for Education Statistics (NCES) Recent College Graduates Survey conflicted with the findings from the NSF data. Specifically, the economic returns to general liberal arts college graduates were significantly lower than to graduates of comprehensive universities but were higher than the earnings of graduates at research universities.

The relationship between institutional type and earnings has been of interest to a number of researchers in the last several years (Bellas, 1998; Fitzgerald, 2000;

Monks, 2000, for example) and has remained unclear. Bellas (1998) found that graduates from research and doctoral universities experienced greater earnings than their peers from selective and general liberal arts colleges but that the earnings differences were largely mediated by labor market experience and occupational classification. Yet Monks (2000), controlling for student background characteristics, institutional selectivity, and work experience, found graduates of selective and general liberal arts colleges experienced an earnings disadvantage.

The extent to which economic returns have been found to be inconsistent was further evident in Fitzgerald's study (2000) using the 1991 follow-up of the High School and Beyond 1980 cohort. Fitzgerald found that although women who graduate from a selective liberal arts college reported greater earnings early in their career, men who graduate from a private research university experienced an earnings penalty.

From these studies, it is clear the body of evidence regarding employment-related earnings of attending a liberal arts college (versus another type of institution) is inconclusive. Although past research has focused on the net effects of institutional type on earnings and given that the cost of higher education continues to increase, studies may also need to take into account the average cost associated with different institutional types. Estimating the return on educational investment is an area where more research is needed.

Summary

Although the studies reviewed in previous sections are significant initial contributions to our understanding of the distinctive impacts of liberal arts colleges and liberal arts education, the existing evidence is limited in important ways. First, the studies that do exist tend to be disparate and disconnected, with each focusing on an idiosyncratic aspect of the impact of liberal arts colleges. Consequently, the findings do not easily form a coherent or integrated body of evidence. Second, the body of evidence is based largely on cross-sectional studies that more often than not use student self-reported gains as outcomes measures. Although such cross-sectional investigations can make a substantial contribution, the very nature of cross-sectional studies makes it extremely difficult to control for differential student recruitment and selection effects (Astin and Lee, 2003). It may simply be the case that, compared with other types of institutions, liberal arts colleges attract and enroll students who are more inclined to high levels of academic and social engagement and more receptive to the educational and developmental influences of postsecondary education when they enter college. This major threat to the interval validity of existing evidence tends to be exacerbated when outcomes are measured by means of student self-reported gains (Pascarella, 2001). Moreover, few studies have been conducted with a sample of colleges broad enough to include the extreme variation among liberal arts colleges. For the most part, the largest amount of empirical evidence of the effects of liberal arts colleges on educational outcomes has resulted from comparisons of selective liberal arts colleges (or those granting 50 percent of degrees to students majoring in traditional liberal arts disciplines) with other types of institutions, failing to capture the extreme variation across liberal arts colleges.

This report details the results of a large, systematic study of the short- and long-term impacts of liberal arts colleges and liberal arts education using two longitudinal datasets that together contain information on more than 6,500 students and alumni from more than 40 institutions located throughout the country. The longitudinal nature of both datasets allowed us to carry out analyses in a way that avoids the major methodological problems characteristic of much of the existing research. Specifically, we were able to estimate the net effects of liberal arts colleges while controlling for many potentially biasing influences of different student precollege characteristics—including in many instances a parallel precollege score on the outcome measure. For example, in estimating the effects of liberal arts colleges on intellectual and personal growth during college, we were able to take into account where students scored on each outcome measure when they entered college. Our review of the literature indicates that this report is likely the largest and most comprehensive investigation of the effects of liberal arts colleges and liberal arts education to date.

The Study

THE STUDY WE CONDUCTED sought answers to the following questions:

1. To what extent are liberal arts colleges more effective than other four-year institutions (that is, research universities, regional comprehensive colleges and universities) in fostering empirically validated good practices in undergraduate education?
2. To what extent are liberal arts colleges more effective than other institutions in influencing different dimensions of students' intellectual and personal development during college? To what extent are liberal arts colleges' impacts on student growth explained by the fact that these institutions foster good practices in undergraduate education?
3. To what extent does an institution's emphasis on liberal arts education foster students' intellectual and personal growth during college? That is, do the elements of liberal arts education emphasized by an institution (for example, concern with student development and effective teaching, intellectual challenge and high expectations, an integrated intellectual experience, extensive interaction with faculty and peers) foster student growth irrespective of institutional type?
4. What are the estimated long-term impacts of attending a liberal arts college (versus another type of institution) on one's personal and professional life five years, fifteen years, and twenty-five years after college graduation?
5. To what extent are the estimated net effects of attending a liberal arts college or an institution's liberal arts emphasis general or conditional? That

is, are the estimated effects essentially similar in magnitude and direction for all students (general effects), or do they differ in magnitude and direction for students who differ by race, sex, tested ability, and the like (conditional effects)?

Datasets Analyzed

To obtain answers to the five general questions of the study, we conducted extensive analyses of two longitudinal datasets: the National Study of Student Learning (NSSL) and the Appalachian College Association (ACA) study. The NSSL was funded by the Department of Education and permitted us to follow random samples of students from sixteen four-year colleges and universities for three years. The sixteen institutions in the NSSL varied widely in selectivity—from some of the most selective in the country (for example, average SAT score of 1400) to institutions that were essentially open admission. The student population from the sixteen schools approximated the national population of four-year undergraduates by ethnicity, gender, and age. Five of the institutions were private liberal arts colleges that varied substantially in selectivity and had a median enrollment of 1,707. According to the Carnegie typology at the time of the study, three of the five were designated as selective liberal arts colleges, while two fell into the category of general liberal arts colleges. Three additional institutions were designated by the Carnegie typology as Research I institutions, while one was designated as a Research II institution. Hereafter, this group of four institutions is termed *research universities.* The median enrollment of the research universities was 22,990. The remaining seven institutions fell into Carnegie categories between liberal arts colleges and research universities. They were comprehensive and doctoral-granting institutions with limited graduate programs and a primarily regional mission. The median enrollment at these institutions was 12,478. Hereafter, this group of colleges and universities is termed *regional institutions.*

The NSSL database contains extensive information about students' cognitive and personal development, much of it based on standardized instruments, and measures a wide range of students' academic and nonacademic experiences during each of the three years of the study. The information was collected from each student participant in the NSSL on four separate occasions: at entrance to college, and at the end of the first, second, and third years of college. Students' academic and nonacademic experiences were collected from their responses to the CSEQ (Pace, 1990) and an instrument developed specifically for the NSSL. Although the NSSL was conducted nearly a decade ago (1992–1995), it was chosen for this study because of the richness and depth of the data it provides. There are between 500 and 600 variables for each student participant in the NSSL. We are aware of no other longitudinal database in postsecondary education that combines the strength of standardized measures of cognitive and personal development with such extensive information on the particulars of students' academic and nonacademic experiences during college.

The alumni follow-up of the Appalachian College Association study was conducted in 2001 and was funded by the Mellon and Spencer Foundations. The data collection was conducted by the American College Testing (ACT) program. The ACA study follows three separate samples of graduates from twenty-six institutions for five years, fifteen years, and twenty-five years after graduation, respectively. The twenty-six institutions are located in four different states and include ten private, baccalaureate-level liberal arts colleges, eleven private master's level institutions, and five public regional universities. The median enrollment of the baccalaureate-level liberal arts colleges was 1,140, the median enrollment at the master's-granting institutions was 1,630, and the median enrollment at the public regional universities was 8,320. Clearly, the ACA data are limited in generalizability because of their focus on institutions located in the Appalachian region. This fact may be counterbalanced by several strengths, however. A particular strength of the ACA study is that it contains not only an extensive variety of information on graduates' perceptions of college impact and their personal and professional lives but also extensive information on each participating graduate before college (for example, ACT composite score, high school achievement, educational aspirations, and the like). Moreover, because it contains samples of alumni approximately five, fifteen, and twenty-five years after graduation, the ACA data permitted us to determine whether the estimated impacts of liberal arts colleges differed in magnitude over time. Possibly the only other dataset of a similar nature is College and Beyond (Bowen and Bok, 1998), but it focuses on highly selective institutions, so it may be as limited in generalizability as the ACA data.

Sample Descriptions

The core samples for the National Study of Student Learning consisted of 1,957 students through the first follow-up (580 at liberal arts colleges, 544 at research universities, 833 at regional institutions), 1,341 students through the second follow-up (419 at liberal arts colleges, 373 at research universities, 549 at regional institutions), and 936 students through the third follow-up (299 at liberal arts colleges, 259 at research universities, and 378 at regional institutions). These three follow-up samples represent 72.2 percent, 49.5 percent, and 34.6 percent, respectively, of the original random sample of 2,709 entering students at the sixteen institutions in the NSSL. Because of attrition from the original sample over the course of the study, several steps were taken to improve and verify the representativeness of the samples. First, we developed a separate sample weighting algorithm for each of the three years of the study to adjust for potential response bias by sex, ethnicity, and institution. Within each of the sixteen institutions, participants were weighted up to that institution's end-of-year population by sex (that is, male or female), and race or ethnicity (that is, white, black, Hispanic, other). For example, if an institution had 100 Hispanic men in its first-year class and 25 Hispanic men in the sample, each Hispanic male in the first-year sample was assigned a weight of 4.00.

Although applying sample weights in this way corrects for bias in the samples we analyzed by sex, ethnicity, and institution, it cannot adjust for nonresponse bias. We conducted several additional analyses, however, to examine differences in the characteristics of students who participated in all years of the NSSL and those who dropped out of the study. The dropouts consisted of two groups: those who dropped out of the institution during the study and those who persisted at the institution but dropped out of the study. Initial participants who left their respective institutions had somewhat lower levels of precollege cognitive test scores (as measured by fall 1992 scores on the Collegiate Assessment of Academic Proficiency [CAAP] reading comprehension, mathematics, and critical thinking tests), socioeconomic background, and academic motivation than their counterparts who persisted in the study. Yet students who remained in the study and those who dropped out of the study but persisted at the institution differed in only small, chance ways with respect to precollege cognitive test scores, age, race, and socioeconomic background (Pascarella and others, 1998).

The core sample for the ACA study consisted of 5,786 alumni of the twenty-six participating institutions (2,007 at private baccalaureate liberal arts colleges, 1,990 at private master's level institutions, and 1,789 at public regional universities). Overall, the sample represented about 12.6 percent of the population of alumni of the twenty-six institutions who graduated in three cohorts, each spanning three graduating classes: 1974, 1975, 1976 (1974 to 1976 cohort); 1984, 1985, 1986 (1984 to 1986 cohort); and 1994, 1995, 1996 (1994 to 1996 cohort). Using estimated population figures provided by ACT, the alumni sample was weighted up to the total population of alumni of the twenty-six participating institutions by sex and institution, within each of the three graduation cohorts. The weighted sample was quite similar to the estimated population of alumni by sex, race, ACT English and mathematics scores, secondary school grades, precollege education degree plans, and expectations of the need for financial aid during college. The three graduation cohorts were almost equally represented: 33.9 percent of the weighted sample were from the 1974 to 1976 cohort, 31.4 percent from the 1984 to 1986 cohort, and 34.7 percent from the 1994 to 1996 cohort.

One of the major strengths of both the NSSL and ACA data used in this study is that they are longitudinal. The NSSL data not only measured students' experiences and their intellectual and personal development during college but also had extensive background data on all students and collected baseline data on nearly all outcome measures when students entered college. Similarly, the ACA data had extensive background information from alumni when they were in high school and applying to college as well as a number of aspects of graduates' college experiences. Thus, we were able to introduce a wide range of statistical controls for important confounding influences in our estimates of the net effects of liberal arts colleges, an institution's liberal arts emphasis, or students' liberal arts experiences.

The importance of introducing statistical controls for potential confounding influences in estimating the net impact of attending a liberal arts college (versus another type of institution) was underscored in comparisons of the precollege characteristics of students attending different types of institutions. For example, in the NSSL data, students attending liberal arts colleges (as compared with students attending both national research universities or regional institutions) were significantly more likely to be attending their college of first choice and to come from families with significantly higher parental income and education. Compared with their counterparts at both research universities and regional institutions, liberal arts college students also had significantly higher levels of secondary school extracurricular involvement and volunteer activities as well as significantly higher precollege levels of critical thinking skills, openness to diversity and challenge, orientation toward learning for self-understanding, and preference for higher-order cognitive tasks. During the first year of college, liberal arts college students were more likely than students at the other types of institutions to live on campus and attend college full time. They were also more likely than students at other institutions to take courses in the arts, humanities, and social sciences and less likely to take courses in mathematics, science, and technical or preprofessional areas. Similarly, in the ACA data, alumni of baccalaureate liberal arts colleges had significantly higher ACT scores, were significantly more likely to be white, and to come from families with significantly higher levels of formal education than alumni of public regional universities. In short, the liberal arts colleges in our samples tended to recruit and enroll students with significantly different family backgrounds and precollege characteristics than other types of institutions. Failure to take such precollege differences into account could easily lead one to confuse a differential recruitment effect for a differential institutional impact.

Effects of Liberal Arts Colleges on Good Practices in Undergraduate Education

THIS CHAPTER SUMMARIZES FINDINGS addressing the question of whether or not liberal arts colleges foster good practices in undergraduate education.

Data and Analyses

To answer this question, we conducted extensive analyses of the NSSL database. The richness of the NSSL data permitted us to construct measures of student-reported good practices that were guided by Chickering and Gamson's principles (1987, 1991) of good practice in undergraduate education and additional research on effective teaching, influential peer interactions, and supportive campus environments (Astin, 1993; Davis and Murrell, 1993; Feldman, 1997; Pascarella and Terenzini, 1991; Whitt and others, 1999). Twenty-one measures or scales of "good practices" were grouped in the following eight general categories:

1. *Student-faculty contact:* quality of nonclassroom interactions with faculty, faculty interest in teaching, and student development;
2. *Cooperation among students:* instructional emphasis on cooperative learning, course-related interaction with peers;
3. *Active learning/time on task:* academic effort or involvement, essay exams in courses, instructors' use of higher-order questioning techniques, emphasis on higher-order examination questions, computer use;
4. *Prompt feedback:* instructors' feedback to students;

5. *High expectations:* course challenge or effort, scholarly and intellectual emphasis, number of textbooks or assigned readings, number of term papers or written reports;

6. *Quality of teaching:* instructional clarity, instructional organization and preparation;

7. *Influential interactions with other students:* quality of interactions with students, non-course-related interactions with peers, cultural and interpersonal involvement, extracurricular involvement;

8. *Supportive campus environment:* emphasis on supportive interactions with others.

Information on all twenty-one good practice measures was collected at the end of the first, second, and third years of college. Detailed operational definitions of all variables and, where appropriate, scale reliabilities are shown in Part A of Appendix A.

Extensive evidence exists to indicate that, even in the presence of controls for important confounding influences, the good practice dimensions measured in this investigation are significantly and positively linked to desired cognitive and noncognitive growth during college (Astin, 1993; Chickering and Reisser, 1993; Kuh, Schuh, Whitt, and Associates, 1991; Pascarella and Terenzini, 1991, 2005). Examples of individual studies supporting the predictive validity of specific dimensions of good practices operationalized in this investigation include *student-faculty contact* (Anaya, 1999; Frost, 1991; Kuh and Hu, 1999; Terenzini and others, 1994); *cooperation among students* (Cabrera and others, 2002; Johnson, Johnson, and Smith, 1998a, 1998b; Qin, Johnson, and Johnson, 1995; Terenzini and others, 2001); *active learning/time on task* (Astin, 1993; Ethington, 1998; Grayson, 1999; Hagedorn, Siadat, Nora, and Pascarella, 1997; Hake, 1998; Johnstone, Ashbaugh, and Warfield, 2002; Kuh, Pace, and Vesper, 1997; Watson and Kuh, 1996); *high expectations* (Arnold, Kuh, Vesper, and Schuh, 1993; Astin, 1993; Bray, Pascarella, and Pierson, 2004; Whitmire and Lawrence, 1996); *quality of teaching and prompt feedback* (d'Apollonia and Abrami, 1997; Feldman, 1994, 1997; Hines, Cruickshank, and Kennedy, 1985; Pascarella and others, 1996a; Wood and Murray, 1999); *influential interactions with other students* (Astin, 1993; Davis and Murrell, 1993;

Douzenis, 1996; Inman and Pascarella, 1998; Volkwein and Carbone, 1994; Whitt and others, 1999); and *supportive campus environment* (Carini and Kuh, 2003; Davis and Murrell, 1993; Graham, 1998; Kuh, Pace, and Vesper, 1997).

To estimate the unique or net effects of attending a liberal arts college (versus a research university or a regional institution) on good practices in undergraduate education, we conducted several sets of multiple regression analyses. In the first set of analyses, each of the twenty-one good practice dimensions, aggregated across the first two years of the NSSL study, was regressed on categorical variables representing attendance at a liberal arts college (versus another type of institution) and all of the control variables shown in Part A of Appendix B (that is, student precollege characteristics, living on or off campus, full- or part-time enrollment, and a measure of the tested academic ability [or selectivity] of each institution's student body). In the second set of analyses, we tested for the presence of conditional effects of liberal arts college attendance by sex, race, tested academic ability, parental education, and level of secondary school involvement. That is, does the evidence suggest that liberal arts colleges have the same influence on good practices for all students (general effects), or are these institutions differentially influential for different kinds of students (conditional effects)?

In a final set of analyses, we estimated the net impact of attending a liberal arts college on the twenty-one good practice dimensions in each of the three years of the NSSL study. In the second and third years, controls were also introduced for students' scores on each good practice dimension in the preceding years. This approach permitted us to estimate not only the net impact on good practices of the first year of attendance at a liberal arts college but also the incremental increase in the effect of attending a liberal arts college in successive years.

Results

Our estimates of the unique or net effects of attending a liberal arts college (versus a national research university or a regional college or university) on demonstrated good practices in undergraduate education are summarized in Table 1. The findings summarized in that table reflect student reports of good

TABLE 1

Significant Estimated Effects of Attending a Liberal Arts College (versus a National Research University or a Regional College or University) on Good Practices in Undergraduate Education Across Two Years of College

Good Practice Variable	Liberal Arts Colleges versus Research Universities				Liberal Arts Colleges versus Regional Institutions			
	Total Effect[a]		Direct Effect[b]		Total Effect[a]		Direct Effect[b]	
	B[c]	Effect Size[d]	B[c]	Effect Size[d]	B[c]	Effect Size[d]	B[c]	Effect Size[d]
Student-faculty contact								
Quality of nonclassroom interactions with faculty	5.707	.866	5.370	.815	3.614	.548	2.763	.419
Faculty interest in teaching and student development	4.405	.772	4.326	.759	2.286	.401	1.925	.338
Cooperation among students								
Instructional emphasis on cooperative learning	1.532	.360	1.329	.312	1.218	.286		
Active learning/time on task								
Academic effort involvement	7.642	.274	8.258	.296	9.033	.323	10.078	.361
Essay exams in courses	.938	.584			.882	.550		
Instructor's use of higher-order examination questions	2.732	.675	2.654	.655	1.899	.469	1.458	.360
Emphasis on higher-order examination questions	2.432	.525	2.345	.506	1.756	.379		
Computer use	1.375	.384	1.125	.286				
Prompt feedback								
Instructor feedback to students	.753	.519	.763	.526				

High expectations

Course challenge/effort	2.565	.550	2.480	.532	2.337	.502	1.454	.312
Number of textbooks or assigned readings	.443	.301	.360	.245	.669	.455		
Number of term papers or written assignments	1.056	.668	.918	.581	1.287	.814	.926	.586
Scholarly/intellectual emphasis	1.822	.370	2.094	.426	1.398	.284		
Quality of teaching								
Instructional skill/clarity	2.604	.537	2.903	.599	1.122	.231	1.687	.348
Instructional organization/preparation	1.860	.425	2.086	.476	1.407	.321		
Influential interactions with other students								
Quality of interactions with students	3.519	.389			4.951	.548		
Non-course-related interactions with peers	2.430	.269			4.036	.447		
Cultural and interpersonal involvement					8.471	.272		
Extracurricular involvement	9.540	.338			14.971	.531		
Supportive campus environment								
Emphasis on supportive interactions with others	3.355	.615	3.402	.624	2.083	.382	1.917	.352

[a]Equations also include controls for tested precollege academic ability (composite of CAAP reading comprehension, mathematics, and critical thinking test scores); the average tested precollege academic ability (composite of CAAP reading comprehension, mathematics and critical thinking test scores), or selectivity, of students entering each institution; precollege educational plans; a measure of precollege academic motivation; whether or not the college attended was one's first choice; age; sex; race; parents' education and income; secondary school grades; time spent during high school working for pay; a scale consisting of time spent during high school in seven activities (studying, socializing with friends, talking with teachers outside class, exercising or sports, studying with friends, volunteer work, and extracurricular activities).

[b]Equations also include all the controls shown in note *a* plus on-campus residence and cumulative number of credit hours completed.

[c]Unstandardized regression coefficient is the average, statistically adjusted difference between liberal arts college students and comparison institution students on each good practice variable. A positive sign means that liberal arts colleges have a higher adjusted score on the variable.

[d]The "effect size" is computed by dividing the regression coefficient by the pooled standard deviation of the good practice variable and indicates that fraction of a standard deviation that liberal arts college students are advantaged or disadvantaged (depending on the sign) relative to comparison institution students.

practices aggregated across the first two years of college; only statistically significant effects are shown. (Here, and for all results shown in the rest of the report, the estimates are based on weighted samples with statistical significance set at no greater than $p < .05$.) As the table further indicates, we estimated two types of effects—"total" and "direct." The "Total Effect" columns in Table 1 show the estimated impact of attending a liberal arts college (versus another type of institution) on each good practice dimension, statistically adjusted for an extensive battery of student precollege characteristics and a measure of the academic selectivity of the college's student body (see footnote a in the table). Although the total effect estimates the impact of liberal arts colleges on good practices independent of student precollege characteristics and institutional selectivity, it still includes the confounding, or mediating, effects of subsequent influences associated with attending a liberal arts college (Alwin and Hauser, 1975): living on campus and full-time attendance. The "Direct Effects" columns in Table 1 show the estimated impacts of liberal arts colleges, controlling not only for student precollege characteristics and college selectivity but also for living on campus (versus off campus and commuting to college) and a measure of full-time enrollment (cumulative number of credit hours completed). The B, or metric regression coefficients, in Table 1 represent the statistically adjusted mean difference between liberal arts college students and their counterparts at other institutions on each good practice variable. The "Effect Size" columns in the table put each of these mean differences on a common scale: the standard deviation of each good practice variable. Thus, an effect size of .80 indicates that liberal arts colleges have a net advantage over comparison institutions on a specific good practice dimension of .80 of a standard deviation. Conversely, an effect size of $-.80$ would mean liberal arts colleges are at a similar net disadvantage.

Two trends are immediately apparent from an inspection of Table 1. First, with statistical controls in place for important confounding influences, statistically significant net differences existed between liberal arts colleges and other institutions on twenty of the twenty-one measures of good practices assessed in the NSSL data. Only on the course-related interaction with peers scale were the differences between liberal arts colleges and other institutions nonsignificant. Second, in all cases where statistically significant net differences were uncovered, students attending liberal arts colleges reported higher levels of good practices across the first two years of college than did their peers attending either research universities or regional institutions.

Total Effects

Liberal arts colleges had an extensive number of positive total effects on good practices versus both research universities and regional institutions, although the advantage was slightly more pronounced in comparison with the former. Net of student precollege characteristics and student body selectivity, students attending liberal arts colleges reported significantly higher levels of exposure, or engagement in, nineteen of twenty-one good practice dimensions than did their counterparts at research universities. The total effects advantage of liberal arts colleges over research universities ranged from .27 to .87 of a standard deviation, with a median effect size of .52 of a standard deviation. Similarly, students attending liberal arts colleges reported significantly higher levels of exposure to, or engagement in, seventeen of twenty-one good practice dimensions than students at regional institutions. The total effects advantage of liberal arts colleges over regional institutions ranged from .23 to .81 of a standard deviation, with a median effect size of .45 of a standard deviation. The only good practice dimensions on which liberal arts colleges did not demonstrate significant total effect advantage over research universities were course-related interaction with peers and cultural and interpersonal involvement. By comparison, liberal arts colleges demonstrated no statistically significant total effect advantage over regional institutions on four good practice dimensions: course-related interaction with peers, computer use, instructor feedback to students, and instructional organization and preparation.

Direct Effects

Our direct effect equations estimated the impact of liberal arts colleges on good practices that was independent, not only of student precollege characteristics and institutional selectivity (that is, the total effects equations) but also of whether or not a student lived on campus and attended college full time.

Consequently, we anticipated that a number of the positive total effects of attending a liberal arts college would become nonsignificant in our direct effect equations, indicating that those effects were largely the result of the greater tendency of liberal arts college students to live on campus and attend college full time. It did, in fact, happen on several good practice dimensions, particularly those involving influential interactions with other students. Liberal arts colleges had total effect advantages relative to both research universities and regional institutions in quality of interactions with students, non-course-related interactions with peers, and extracurricular involvement. Each of these significant, positive total effects of attendance at a liberal arts college became nonsignificant, however, when living on campus and number of credit hours earned were taken into account. The same held true for the positive total effects of liberal arts colleges (versus regional institutions) on cultural and interpersonal involvement and instructional emphasis on cooperative learning. Much of the positive influence of liberal arts colleges on influential interactions with other students is mediated, or explained, by their residential, full-time character.

At the same time, it is clear that the residential, full-time character of liberal arts colleges does not account for all of their positive influence on good practices in undergraduate education. As Table 1 indicates, liberal arts colleges still had a substantial number of significant, positive direct effects on good practices—although they tended to be fewer in number and, in the comparison of liberal arts colleges with regional institutions, somewhat smaller in magnitude than the positive total effects. Net of living on campus and credit hours earned, as well as precollege characteristics and institutional selectivity, students attending liberal arts colleges reported significantly higher levels of exposure to, or engagement in, fifteen of twenty-one good practice dimensions than did their peers at research universities. The direct effects advantage of liberal arts colleges over research universities ranged from .25 to .82 of a standard deviation, with a median effect size of .53 of a standard deviation. In comparison, students attending liberal arts colleges reported significantly higher levels of exposure to, or engagement in, nine of twenty-one good practice dimensions than did students attending regional institutions. The direct effects advantage of liberal arts colleges over regional institutions ranged from .31 to .59 of a standard deviation, with a median effect size of .35.

Perhaps the most striking finding was that liberal arts colleges had a significant direct effect advantage over both research universities and regional institutions on nine of twenty-one good practice dimensions, including both measures of *student-faculty contact* (quality of nonclassroom interactions with faculty and faculty interest in teaching and student development); two of five measures of *active learning/time on task* (academic effort and involvement and instructors' use of higher-order questioning techniques); two of five measures of *high expectations* (course challenge/effort and number of term papers or written reports); both measures of *quality of teaching* (instructional skill and clarity and instructional organization and preparation); and the single measure of *supportive campus environment* (emphasis on supportive interactions with others). On these dimensions of good practices, the positive impact of attending a liberal arts college (relative to both research universities and regional institutions) was independent, not only of student precollege characteristics and institutional selectivity but also of living on campus and attending college full time.

Conditional Effects

Our analyses of conditional effects in the prediction of good practices in undergraduate education considered sex, race, age, tested precollege academic preparation, and level of high school extracurricular involvement. In none of those analyses did we find evidence of statistically significant conditional effects. This finding supported a conclusion that the estimated effects of attending a liberal arts college (versus another type of institution) on good practices in undergraduate education tended to be general rather than conditional. That is, the estimated impacts of liberal arts colleges summarized in Table 1 tend to be of similar magnitude for men and women, for white students and students of color, for students of different ages, and for students with different levels of tested academic ability and high school extracurricular involvement.

Timing of Effects

Our final set of analyses sought to estimate the incremental, direct impact of liberal arts colleges on good practices for each of the three years of the study. Thus, in estimating the unique effect of attending a liberal arts college on any good practice dimension in the second and third year, we included not only controls for precollege characteristics, institutional selectivity, living on campus, and full-time enrollment but also controls for one's score on that good practice dimension in the previous year. Doing so permitted us to estimate the unique impact on good practices of each succeeding year of attendance at a liberal arts college. The results of these analyses are summarized in Table 2. Part A of Table 2 shows the net direct effects of attendance at a liberal arts college during the first year of college on good practices. As the table indicates, students attending liberal arts colleges reported a significantly higher level on sixteen of twenty-one good practices than did students at research universities and a significantly higher level on thirteen of twenty-one good practices than did their counterparts at regional institutions. The median advantage of liberal arts colleges over research universities was .41 of a standard deviation, while the corresponding advantage of liberal arts colleges over regional institutions was slightly smaller, .32 of a standard deviation.

Part B of Table 2 shows the estimated incremental contribution of the second year of attendance at a liberal arts college on good practices. (Recall in these analyses that, in addition to all other statistical controls, a student's first-year score on each good practice dimension was also incorporated into the regression specification.) As Part B of Table 2 indicates, net of other influences, students attending liberal arts colleges reported significantly higher levels on ten of twenty-one good practices than did similar students at research universities and a significantly higher level on five of twenty-one good practices then did their counterparts at regional institutions. The median advantage of liberal arts colleges over research universities was .23 of a standard deviation, while the corresponding advantage of liberal arts colleges over regional institutions was .19 of a standard deviation.

Part C of Table 2 shows the estimated incremental contribution of the third year of attendance at a liberal arts college on good practices. (Recall in these analyses that, in addition to all other statistical controls, a student's cumulative first- and second-year score on each good practice dimension was also included in the regression specification.) As Part B of the table indicates, the trend of fewer and smaller effects from the first to the second year of college continued from the second to the third year. Net of other influences,

TABLE 2
Statistically Significant Estimated Effects of Attending a Liberal Arts College (versus a Research University or Regional Institution) on Good Practices in Undergraduate Education for Each Year of the Study[a]

Good Practice Variable	Liberal Arts Colleges versus Research Universities		Liberal Arts Colleges versus Regional Institutions	
	Metric Regression Coefficient[b]	Effect Size[c]	Metric Regression Coefficient[b]	Effect Size[c]
Part A: First Year of College				
Student-faculty contact				
Quality of nonclassroom interactions with faculty	2.211	.590	1.092	.291
Faculty interest in teaching and student development	1.814	.570	.783	.246
Cooperation among students				
Instructional emphasis on cooperative learning	.496	.186	.586	.206
Active learning/time on task				
Academic effort/involvement	4.893	.330	6.460	.486
Number of essay exams in courses	.395	.386		
Instructor's use of higher-order questioning techniques	1.415	.544	.986	.412
Emphasis on higher-order examination questions	1.073	.396	.665	.245
Computer use	.910	.389		
Prompt feedback				
Instructor feedback to students	.778	.542	.348	.243
High expectations				
Course challenge/effort	1.313	.476	.982	.356
Number of textbooks or assigned readings	.318	.360	.284	.322
Number of term papers or written reports	.425	.421	.458	.453
Scholarly/intellectual emphasis			.953	.323

(Continued)

TABLE 2 (*Continued*)

Good Practice Variable	Liberal Arts Colleges versus Research Universities		Liberal Arts Colleges versus Regional Institutions	
	Metric Regression Coefficient[b]	Effect Size[c]	Metric Regression Coefficient[b]	Effect Size[c]
Quality of teaching				
Instructional skill/clarity	1.304	.466	.896	.316
Instructional organization/preparation	.891	.347	.876	.341
Influential interactions with other students				
Extracurricular involvement	3.162	.206		
Supportive campus environment				
Emphasis on supportive interactions with others	1.725	.500		
Part B: Second Year of College				
Student-faculty contact				
Quality of nonclassroom interactions with faculty	2.273	.345	1.205	.183
Faculty interest in teaching and student development	1.725	.303	1.069	.188
Cooperation among students				
Instructional emphasis on cooperative learning	.629	.148		
Active learning/time on task				
Number of essay exams in courses	.463	.288		
Instructor's use of higher-order questioning techniques	.679	.168		
Emphasis on higher-order examination questions	1.085	.234		
Prompt feedback				
Instructor feedback to students	.522	.360		
High expectations				
Number of term papers or written reports	.404	.256	.385	.244
Scholarly/intellectual emphasis			.703	.143
Quality of teaching				
Instructional skill/clarity	.614	.127		
Supportive campus environment				
Emphasis on supportive interactions with others	1.266	.232	1.124	.207

TABLE 2 (*Continued*)

	Liberal Arts Colleges versus Research Universities		Liberal Arts Colleges versus Regional Institutions	
Good Practice Variable	Metric Regression Coefficient[b]	Effect Size[c]	Metric Regression Coefficient[b]	Effect Size[c]
Part C: Third Year of College				
Student-faculty contact				
Faculty interest in teaching and student development	1.209	.142		
Cooperation among students				
Instructional emphasis on cooperative learning	.831	.140		
Active learning/time on task				
Academic effort/involvement			5.083	.135
Number of essay exams in courses	.298	.136		
Instructor's use of higher-order questioning techniques	.658	.118		
Prompt feedback				
Instructor feedback to students	.580	.414		
Quality of teaching				
Instructional skill/clarity	.930	.131		
Supportive campus environment				
Emphasis on supportive interactions with others	1.020	.131		

[a]Equations also include controls for tested precollege academic ability (composite of CAAP reading comprehension, mathematics, and critical thinking test scores); the average tested precollege academic ability (composite of CAAP reading comprehension, mathematics, and critical thinking test scores) of students entering each institution; precollege educational plans; a measure of precollege academic motivation; whether or not the college attended was one's first choice; age; sex; race; parents' education and income; secondary school grades; time spent during secondary school in eight separate activities (studying, socializing with friends, talking with teachers outside class, working for pay, exercising or sports, studying with friends, volunteer work, and extracurricular activities); on-campus versus off-campus residence; and cumulative number of credit hours completed. In the second-year analyses, each equation also included a student's first-year score on each good practice variable. In the third-year analyses, each equation also included a student's cumulative first- and second-year score on each good practice variable.
[b]The metric regression coefficient represents the average difference between liberal arts college students and comparison institution students on each good practice variable, statistically adjusted for the controls listed in note *a* above.
[c]The effect size is computed by dividing the metric regression coefficient by the pooled standard deviation of the good practice variable and indicates that fraction of a standard deviation that liberal arts college students are advantaged or disadvantaged (depending on the sign) relative to the comparison institution students.

students attending liberal arts colleges reported significantly higher levels on seven of twenty-one good practices than did their counterparts at research universities and a significantly higher level on only one of twenty-one good practices than did similar students at regional institutions. The median advantage of liberal arts colleges over both research universities and regional institutions was only .14 of a standard deviation.

The conclusion suggested by the evidence summarized in Table 2 is that the advantages liberal arts colleges demonstrated in promoting good practices in undergraduate education were most pronounced in the initial year of postsecondary education. Thereafter, the incremental contribution of each additional year of attendance at a liberal arts college over previous years became less broadly based and smaller in magnitude. This diminishing returns relationship does not mean, however, that the emphasis on promoting good practices in undergraduate education at liberal arts colleges is any less salient in the second and third years of postsecondary education than it is in the first year. Our analytical approach was designed to estimate the incremental, or additional, contribution to good practices attributable to each successive year of attendance at a liberal arts college. Thus, what our findings indicate is that liberal arts colleges have their most pronounced impact on good practices in undergraduate education in the initial year of college. Thereafter, liberal arts colleges continue to significantly promote good practices above and beyond their first-year impacts, but their additional, positive contributions in subsequent years become fewer in number and smaller in magnitude over time.

Effects of Liberal Arts Colleges on Intellectual and Personal Development

TO WHAT EXTENT DO LIBERAL ARTS COLLEGES enhance student intellectual and personal development?

Data and Analyses

To answer this question, we conducted further analyses of the NSSL data. Using the NSSL data, we estimated the effects of liberal arts colleges on eleven different measures of intellectual and personal growth during college, including five standardized measures of learning and cognitive development, a measure of students' plans to obtain a graduate degree, and five measures of students' orientations toward learning and intellectual pursuits. The five standardized measures of learning and cognitive growth were the five constituent tests of the Collegiate Assessment of Academic Proficiency developed by ACT to assess general cognitive skills typically acquired during college (American College Testing Program, 1990). The tests were each forty minutes long and measured reading comprehension, mathematics, critical thinking, writing skills, and science reasoning, respectively. The reading comprehension, mathematics, and critical thinking tests were each administered when students entered college and at the end of the first year of college. The writing skills and science reasoning tests were administered at the end of the second year of college, and the reading comprehension and critical thinking tests were readministered at the end of the third year of college. Brief descriptions of the content of each CAAP test as well as applicable psychometric properties are shown in Part B of Appendix A.

Plans to obtain a graduate degree was a variable constructed from students' responses to a single item asking them to indicate the "highest academic degree you intend to obtain in your lifetime." Responses were recoded so that 1 = master's degree or above and 0 = bachelor's degree or below. Information on graduate degree plans was obtained when students entered college and again after the first, second, and third years of college.

Students' orientations toward learning and intellectual pursuits were five scales developed for the NSSL that measured openness to diversity and challenge, learning for self-understanding, internal locus of attribution for academic success, preference for higher-order cognitive tasks, and positive attitude toward literacy. Detailed operational definitions of all five scales, along with scale reliabilities, are also shown in Part B of Appendix A. The content validity and predictive validity of the five scales have been indicated in several studies (for example, Pascarella and others, 1996a; Pascarella and others, 1996b; Pierson, Wolniak, Pascarella, and Flowers, 2003; Springer and others, 1996; Whitt and others, 2001; Wolniak, Pierson, and Pascarella, 2001). All five orientations toward learning and intellectual pursuits were assessed when students entered college and again after the first, second, and third years of college. Exhibit 1 summarizes all measures of intellectual and personal growth during college assessed by the study and indicates when the instruments were administered.

Our analyses of the net effects of attending a liberal arts college (versus a research university or regional institution) on measures of intellectual and personal development during college were conducted in three stages. In the first stage, each measure of intellectual or personal development was regressed on categorical variables representing attendance at a liberal arts college (versus another type of institution) and all of the appropriate controls shown in Part B of Appendix B (that is, student precollege characteristics and test scores, and a measure of the tested academic ability [or selectivity] of an institution's student body). (Logistic regression was used in the prediction of graduate degree plans, while ordinary least-squares regression was used in the prediction of all other outcomes.) Doing so provided an estimate of the net total effect of attending a liberal arts college on each outcome (Alwin and Hauser, 1975). The second stage of the analyses (direct effects) sought to estimate the extent to which the total effect of attending a liberal arts college was mediated or

EXHIBIT 1
Measures of Intellectual and Personal Development During College Assessed by the Study (NSSL Data)[a]

Measure(s)/(When Administered)

CAAP Reading Comprehension Test
CAAP Critical Thinking Test
    (Administered at entrance to college and at the end of the first and third years of college)

CAAP Mathematics Test
    (Administered at entrance to college and at the end of the first year of college)

CAAP Science Reasoning Test
CAAP Writing Skills Test
    (Administered at the end of the second year of college)

Plans to Obtain a Graduate Degree
Openness to Diversity and Challenge
Learning for Self-Understanding
Internal Locus of Attribution for Academic Success
Preference for Higher-Order Cognitive Tasks
Positive Attitude Toward Literacy
    (Administered at entrance to college and at the end of the first, second, and third years of college)

[a]Detailed operational definitions of all tests and scales are shown in Appendix A (Part B).

explained by distinctive student experiences at those institutions. In this second stage, we added an extensive set of college experience measures to the stage one (total effects) equations. These college experience measures included all the good practice variables plus on-campus residence, number of credit hours completed, courses taken in five areas (social sciences, mathematics, technical and preprofessional, arts and humanities, natural sciences), college grades, on- and off-campus work responsibilities, Greek affiliation, and participation in intercollegiate athletics. If a significant effect of attending a liberal arts college in the stage one analyses were reduced to nonsignificance, in the stage two analyses it would indicate that the effects of attending a liberal arts college on

TABLE 3

Significant Estimated Effects of Attending a Liberal Arts College (versus a National Research University or a Regional College or University) on Intellectual and Personal Development (NSSL Data)[a]

Outcome	Liberal Arts Colleges versus Research Universities				Liberal Arts Colleges versus Regional Institutions			
	Total Effect[b]		Direct Effect[c]		Total Effect[b]		Direct Effect[c]	
	B[d]	Effect Size[e]	B[d]	Effect Size[e]	B[d]	Effect Size[e]	B[d]	Effect Size[e]
Part A: First Year of College								
Mathematics	−.973	−.215	−.477	−.106	−.522	−.115		
Openness to diversity and challenge	1.097	.223			1.001	.204		
Learning for self-understanding	.518	.243	.426	.200	.283	.133		
Preference for higher-order cognitive tasks	.287	.161						
Positive attitude toward literacy							−.537	−.174
Part B: Second Year of College								
Writing skills	−.861	−.179			.716	.145		
Science reasoning					.824	.164		
Openness to diversity and challenge	1.213	.242						
Learning for self-understanding	.588	.280	.486	.231				
Preference for higher-order cognitive tasks							−.351	−.202

Part C: Third Year of College

Openness to diversity and challenge	1.584	.321
Learning for self-understanding	.700	.335
Positive attitude toward literacy	1.081	.240

[a]No significant net effects of liberal arts colleges were found for first-year graduate degree plans, reading comprehension, critical thinking, internal locus of attribution for academic success; second-year graduate degree plans, internal locus of attribution for academic success, positive attitude toward literacy; or third-year graduate degree plans, reading comprehension, critical thinking, preference for higher-order cognitive tasks, and internal locus of attribution for academic success.

[b]Equations include controls for tested precollege academic ability (composite of CAAP reading comprehension, mathematics, and critical thinking) or a parallel pretest for the prediction of first-year reading comprehension, mathematics, or critical thinking; the average tested precollege academic ability or "selectivity" (composite of CAAP reading comprehension, mathematics, and critical thinking) of students at the institution attended; precollege plans to obtain a graduate degree; precollege academic motivation; college attended was first choice; age; sex; race; parents' income; parents' education; secondary school grades; time spent during high school working for pay; a scale consisting of time spent during high school in seven activities (studying, socializing with friends, talking with teachers outside class, exercising or sports, studying with friends, volunteer work, and extracurricular activities); and an exact parallel precollege measure of each end-of-first-year dependent variable.

[c]Equations include all controls shown in note *b* plus on-campus residence; number of credit hours completed; average hours per week spent studying; courses taken in five areas (social sciences, mathematics, technical/preprofessional, arts and humanities, natural sciences); college grades; instructional skill/clarity; instructional organization/preparation; course challenge/effort; instructional emphasis on cooperative learning; instructor's use of higher-order questioning techniques; emphasis on higher-order examination questions; course-related interaction with peers; academic effort/involvement; science effort/involvement; using computers; number of textbooks or assigned books read; number of nonassigned books read; number of essay exams in courses; number of term papers or other written reports; on-campus work; off-campus work; participated in intercollegiate athletics; Greek affiliation; non-course-related interaction with peers; extracurricular involvement; cultural and interpersonal involvement; volunteer work; quality of nonclassroom interactions with faculty; faculty interest in teaching and student development; scholarly/intellectual emphasis; supportive relationships.

[d]Unstandardized regression coefficient is the average difference between liberal arts college students and comparison institution students on the dependent variable. A positive sign means that liberal arts college students have a higher adjusted score on the variable, while a negative sign means they have a lower adjusted score on the variable.

[e]The "effect size" is computed by dividing the regression coefficient by the pooled standard deviation of the dependent variable and indicates that fraction of a standard deviation that liberal arts college students are advantaged or disadvantaged (depending on the sign) relative to the comparison institution students.

that outcome were largely explained by the distinctive student academic and nonacademic experiences fostered by liberal arts colleges. In the third stage of the analyses, we conducted tests for the presence of conditional effects, considering students' background characteristics such as sex, race, precollege scores on each measure of intellectual or personal development, and the like.

Results

Our estimates of the net effects of attending a liberal arts college (versus a national research university or a regional institution) on measures of intellectual and personal development are summarized in Table 3. The analyses in Table 3 reflect estimated impacts of liberal arts colleges during the first, second, and third years of postsecondary education; only total and direct effects that were statistically significant are shown. The "Total Effect" columns in Table 3 indicate the estimated impact of attending a liberal arts college (versus another type of institution) on each measure of intellectual or personal development, statistically adjusted for students' precollege characteristics and institutional selectivity (see footnote b in the table). The "Direct Effect" columns in Table 3 show the estimated impacts of liberal arts colleges, controlling not only for students' precollege characteristics and institutional selectivity but also for measures of good practices in undergraduate education and other college experiences (see footnote c in the table). Thus, if a significant total effect of liberal arts colleges becomes a nonsignificant direct effect, it indicates that the influence of attending a liberal arts college is accounted for by the good practices in undergraduate education and other collegiate experiences uniquely fostered by these institutions.

It is worth noting that in all analyses, we were able to include among our statistical controls a parallel precollege score (or its proxy) on each outcome measure. Because such pretest measures typically have strong correlations with an outcome or posttest score, they substantially reduce the residual variance in an outcome measure that can be explained by other variables in the prediction model (Pascarella and Terenzini, 1991). Consequently, the results summarized in Table 3 tend to be quite conservative estimates of the net impact of liberal arts colleges. That having been said, liberal arts colleges still demonstrated a number of significant net effects on measures of intellectual and personal development. The effects were most pronounced in comparison with research universities, however, and were not always positive.

Total Effects

As indicated in Table 3, liberal arts colleges had their most consistent positive total effects on students' growth in openness to diversity and challenge and learning for self-understanding. Net of students' precollege characteristics and institutional selectivity, students at liberal arts colleges had significantly higher end-of-first-, second- and third-year openness to diversity and challenge scores than did their counterparts at research universities and higher end-of-first- and second-year scores than did students at regional institutions. Similarly, liberal arts college students demonstrated significantly higher end-of-first-, second-, and third-year learning for self-understanding scores than their research university peers and higher end-of-first-year scores than students at regional institutions. Because our regression specifications included precollege scores on both openness to diversity and learning for self-understanding, these results are conceptually the equivalent of saying that liberal arts college students demonstrated significantly greater net gains in openness to diversity and challenge and learning for self-understanding than did students at either research universities or regional institutions (Pascarella, Wolniak, and Pierson, 2003).

As previously indicated, students attending liberal arts colleges began postsecondary education with significantly higher levels of openness to diversity and learning for self-understanding than did students in the sample who enrolled in research universities or regional institutions. Consequently, because of regression artifacts, one might expect them to have smaller average gains on these measures during college than their peers at other types of institutions who had lower average precollege scores. Yet that is the exact opposite of what happened; net of other influences, liberal arts college students made greater average gains in both openness to diversity and learning for self-understanding than did their counterparts at other institutions. On these dimensions of development, liberal arts colleges functioned to even further accentuate initially high levels of precollege traits that tended to characterize the students they enrolled. Such self-selection and accentuation were also suggested by the first-year advantage of liberal arts college students over students at research universities in preference for higher-order cognitive tasks. Students at liberal arts colleges not only entered postsecondary education with a significantly higher score on this measure than their peers at research universities but also demonstrated significantly larger first-year gains on it.

Two other positive total effects were linked to attendance at a liberal arts college. Statistically controlling for precollege characteristics and institutional selectivity, liberal arts college students evidenced significantly higher net three-year gains in positive attitude toward literacy than did their peers at research universities. Similarly, they demonstrated significantly higher end-of-second-year scores on the CAAP writing skills test than did students at regional institutions.

Not all the total effects of liberal arts colleges were positive. Net of other influences, students at liberal arts colleges made significantly less progress in the development of mathematics skills than did their counterparts at both research universities and regional institutions. Compared with students at research universities, liberal arts college students also were significantly disadvantaged in end-of-second-year science reasoning.

Finally, it is important to point out that there were four dimensions of intellectual and personal development on which we found an essential parity between liberal arts college students and their peers at other institutions. When students' precollege characteristics and institutional selectivity were held constant, only chance differences were found between students attending liberal arts colleges and students attending research universities and regional institutions in CAAP reading comprehension and critical thinking scores, internal locus of attribution for academic success, and plans for a graduate degree.

Direct Effects

As the "Direct Effect" columns in Table 3 show, about 85 percent (ten of twelve) of the positive total effects of liberal arts colleges on measures of intellectual and personal development became nonsignificant when measures of good practices in undergraduate education and other college experiences were added to controls for students' precollege characteristics and institutional selectivity. This finding suggests that most of the net positive influences of liberal arts colleges on students' intellectual and personal development during college are accounted for by the distinctive ability of liberal arts colleges to foster good educational practices and other developmentally enriching experiences during college. The only exception was the positive direct effect advantage of liberal arts college students over their counterparts at research universities on end-of-first- and second-year learning for self-understanding. During the first two years of postsecondary education, the distinctive academic and nonacademic experiences of liberal arts college students did not explain all of the significant positive impact of liberal arts colleges on this dimension. By the end of the third year of college, however, differences in the cumulative three-year academic and nonacademic experiences of students attending liberal arts colleges and their research university peers did, in fact, account for the positive influence of liberal arts colleges on growth in learning for self-understanding.

The only other significant direct effects of liberal arts colleges were negative. Compared with their peers at research universities, liberal arts college students demonstrated significantly smaller first-year gains in mathematics skills; this difference could not be totally accounted for by the fact that they took fewer mathematics and science courses during the first year of college. Similarly, compared with their counterparts at regional institutions, liberal arts college students also made smaller first-year gains in positive attitude toward literacy and smaller gains over two years in preference for higher-order cognitive tasks. These smaller gains could not be explained by students' precollege characteristics and institutional selectivity or by differences between students at liberal arts colleges and regional institutions in the academic and nonacademic experience of college.

Additional Analyses

Recall that three of the five liberal arts colleges in our sample were designated as selective liberal arts colleges, while the remaining two were identified as general liberal arts colleges. Not surprisingly, the three selective liberal arts colleges had "selectivity" estimates (that is, average precollege CAAP reading, mathematics, and critical thinking test scores) that placed them in the upper 25 percent of the distribution of institutions in the NSSL sample. An important line of research on between-institution influences has suggested that it is selective liberal arts colleges that have a particularly powerful influence on the intellectual and personal development of students (for example, Astin, 1999; Chickering, 1969; Chickering and Reisser, 1993; Clark and others, 1972; Heath, 1968; Jacob, 1957; Pascarella and Terenzini, 1991, 1998). To test this possibility with the NSSL data, we took only the three selective liberal arts colleges in our sample and estimated their net total effects on measures of intellectual and personal development versus research universities and regional institutions. To further ascertain the unique contribution of selectivity, we estimated two models: one in which no statistical control was made for selectivity and a second in which our measure of selectivity was specified in the total effects equations. The results of these analyses are summarized in Parts A, B, and C of Table 4. Although the table focuses on statistically significant total effects, several nonsignificant regression equations are presented in parentheses for comparative purposes.

As shown in Table 4, the estimated total effects of attending a selective liberal arts college were quite similar to the total effects summarized in Table 3, where the sample of liberal arts colleges included both selective and nonselective schools. The major difference was that students at selective liberal arts colleges evidenced greater first-year growth in both reading comprehension and critical thinking than did their counterparts at regional institutions. These corresponding differences were nonsignificant when both selective and nonselective liberal arts colleges were the comparison group. It is also worth noting that the academic selectivity of the students enrolled was not a major factor in determining the impacts of selective liberal arts colleges. Controlling for institutional selectivity made a difference in only four of nineteen total effects, and the pattern of influence was inconsistent. In first-year reading comprehension and second-year learning for self-understanding, introducing a control for selectivity reduced a significant positive effect to nonsignificance. On the other two, nonsignificant effects become significant when selectivity was taken into account. Controlling for institutional selectivity, students attending selective liberal arts colleges demonstrated significantly lower first-year

TABLE 4

Significant Estimated Total Effects of Attending a Selective Liberal Arts College (versus a National Research University or a Regional College or University) on Intellectual and Personal Development (NSSL Data)[a]

Outcome	Selective Liberal Arts Colleges versus Research Universities[b]		Selective Liberal Arts Colleges versus Regional Institutions[b]	
	B[c]	Effect Size[d]	B[c]	Effect Size[d]
Part A: First Year of College				
Reading comprehension				
(Selectivity not controlled)[e]			.597	.108
(Selectivity controlled)[f]			(.396)	
Mathematics				
(Selectivity not controlled)[e]	−.854	−.189	(−.105)	
(Selectivity controlled)[f]	−.987	−.218	−.537	−.119
Critical thinking				
(Selectivity not controlled)[e]			.675	.119
(Selectivity controlled)[f]			.719	.126
Openness to diversity and challenge				
(Selectivity not controlled)[e]	1.114	.227	1.187	.242
(Selectivity controlled)[f]	1.044	.213	.921	.118
Learning for self-understanding				
(Selectivity not controlled)[e]	.565	.266	.410	.193
(Selectivity controlled)[f]	.537	.252	.305	.143
Preference for higher-order cognitive tasks				
(Selectivity not controlled)[e]	.253	.142		
(Selectivity controlled)[f]	.260	.146		
Part B: Second Year of College				
Writing skills				
(Selectivity not controlled)[e]			(.563)	
(Selectivity controlled)[f]			.719	.145
Science reasoning				
(Selectivity not controlled)[e]	−1.105	−.231	−.728	−.152
(Selectivity controlled)[f]	−1.131	−.236	−.848	−.177
Openness to diversity and challenge				
(Selectivity not controlled)[e]	1.366	.272	1.333	.266
(Selectivity controlled)[f]	1.233	.256	.932	.186

(Continued)

TABLE 4 (Continued)

Outcome	Selective Liberal Arts Colleges versus Research Universities[b]		Selective Liberal Arts Colleges versus Regional Institutions[b]	
	B[c]	Effect Size[d]	B[c]	Effect Size[d]
Learning for self-understanding				
(Selectivity not controlled)[e]	.667	.317	.391	.186
(Selectivity controlled)[f]	.622	.296	(.180)	
Part C: Third Year of College				
Openness to diversity and challenge				
(Selectivity not controlled)[e]	1.467	.297		
(Selectivity controlled)[f]	1.449	.293		
Learning for self-understanding				
(Selectivity not controlled)[e]	.703	.336		
(Selectivity controlled)[f]	.655	.315		
Positive attitude toward literacy				
(Selectivity not controlled)[e]	1.035	.230		
(Selectivity controlled)[f]	.941	.209		

[a]No significant net effects of selective liberal arts colleges were found for first-year graduate degree plans, internal locus of attribution for academic success, positive attitude toward literacy; second-year graduate degree plans, preference for higher-order cognitive tasks, internal locus of attribution for academic success, positive attitude toward literacy; or third-year graduate degree plans, reading comprehension, critical thinking, preference for higher-order cognitive tasks, and internal locus of attribution for academic success.

[b]Equations include controls for tested precollege academic ability (composite of CAAP reading comprehension, mathematics, and critical thinking) or a parallel pretest for the prediction of third-year reading comprehension or critical thinking; precollege plans to obtain a graduate degree; precollege academic motivation; college attended was first choice; age; sex; race; parents' education; parents' income; secondary school grades; time spent during high school working for pay; a scale consisting of time spent during high school in seven activities (studying, socializing with friends, talking with teachers outside class, exercising or sports, studying with friends, volunteer work, and extracurricular activities); and an exact parallel precollege measure of each end-of-third-year dependent variable.

[c]Unstandardized regression coefficient is the average difference between selective liberal arts college students and comparison institution students on the dependent variable. A positive sign means that liberal arts students at selective colleges have a higher adjusted score on the variable, while a negative sign means they have a lower adjusted score on the variable. (Coefficients in parentheses were nonsignificant.)

[d]The "effect size" is computed by dividing the regression coefficient by the pooled standard deviation of the dependent variable and indicates that fraction of a standard deviation that selective liberal arts college students are advantaged or disadvantaged (depending on the sign) relative to the comparison institution students.

[e]Average tested precollege academic ability, or selectivity (composite of CAAP reading comprehension, mathematics, and critical thinking), of students at the institution attended *not* included in the prediction model.

[f]Average tested precollege academic ability, or selectivity, of students at the institution attended included in the prediction model.

mathematics scores but significantly higher second-year writing skills scores than their peers at regional institutions.

Timing of Impacts

An examination of the total effect estimates and corresponding effect sizes in Tables 3 and 4 indicates that most of the positive impact of liberal arts colleges on measures of students' intellectual and personal development occurred during the first year of exposure to postsecondary education. For example, the significant advantages of students' attending selective liberal arts colleges over their peers at regional institutions in reading comprehension and critical thinking gains occurred only in the first year of college. Similarly, the largest incremental impact of liberal arts colleges (versus research universities) on openness to diversity and learning for self-understanding manifests itself in the first year. Thereafter, the influence of liberal arts colleges increased in magnitude, but the estimated first-year impacts were 69 to 79 percent of the estimated impact at the end of the third year of college. The only outcome on which it was not the case was positive attitude toward literacy. At the end of the first year of college, parity existed between liberal arts colleges and research universities in literacy attitude. By the end of the third year of college, however, students attending liberal arts colleges had an advantage over their research university counterparts of between .20 to .24 of a standard deviation on this dimension. Unlike reading comprehension and critical thinking, which were assessed at the end of the first and third years of college, mathematics was tested only during the first year of college, while science reasoning and writing skills were measured only at the end of the second year. Consequently, it is difficult to form conclusions concerning the timing of the effects of liberal arts colleges on these last three measures.

Conditional Effects

Our analyses of conditional effects in the prediction of measures of intellectual and personal development considered sex, race, age, precollege academic ability, and precollege scores on all outcomes considered. As in our previous analyses predicting exposure to, or engagement in, good practices in undergraduate education, we found little consistent evidence of statistically significant conditional effects. This finding held, irrespective of whether the comparison group was all five liberal arts colleges or only the three selective liberal arts colleges in the NSSL sample. Such evidence supports the conclusion that the estimated effects of attending a liberal arts college or a selective liberal arts college (versus another type of institution) on intellectual and personal development are general rather than conditional. That is, the estimated impacts of liberal arts colleges or selective liberal arts colleges summarized in Tables 3 and 4 tend to be similar in magnitude for men and women, for white students and students of color, for students of different ages, for students with different levels of tested academic ability, and for students who enter college with different pretest scores on each measure of intellectual and personal development considered.

Effects of an Institution's Liberal Arts Emphasis and Students' Liberal Arts Experiences on Intellectual and Personal Development

THIS CHAPTER CONSIDERS THE IMPACT of liberal arts education from a somewhat more complex perspective than simple comparisons based on institutional type (that is, liberal arts colleges versus other institutions).

Data and Analyses

The richness of the NSSL database permitted us to operationalize an institution-level variable that we termed an institution's *liberal arts emphasis.* An institution's liberal arts emphasis is a composite of factors suggested by the literature as salient dimensions of a liberal arts education. These salient dimensions include extensive interaction between students and faculty, faculty emphasis on effective teaching and holistic student development, academic challenge and high expectations, an integrated intellectual experience, an emphasis on coursework in the liberal arts disciplines (for example, humanities, arts, social sciences, natural sciences), a supportive campus environment, an emphasis on a full-time enrollment, residential experience, and extensive student extracurricular involvement and interaction with peers (See, for example, Astin, 1999; Blaich, Bost, Chan, and Lynch, 2004; Heath, 1968; Kimball, 1986; Koblik and Graubard, 2000; Rothblatt, 2003; Winter, McClelland, and Stewart, 1981). Exhibit 2 shows the constituent scales and items for the liberal arts emphasis variable. Two different operational definitions of the variable were considered at the institutional level. The first (Liberal Arts Emphasis I, or LAEMP I) was based solely on the aggregate institutional average of student-reported first-year experiences on fourteen scales and items shown in Exhibit 2. The second operational definition of the liberal arts emphasis variable (Liberal Arts Emphasis II, or LAEMP II) was based on the institutional aggregate of the fourteen student reported experiences plus three institutional characteristics obtained from each of the sixteen participating

EXHIBIT 2
Constituent Scales and Items for the Liberal Arts Emphasis Variables (NSSL Data)

Variable: Liberal Arts Emphasis I (Institutional Level)
  (alpha reliability = .78)
Scale or Item[a]
• Quality of nonclassroom interactions with faculty
• Faculty interest in teaching and student development
• Instructional skill/clarity
• Instructional organization and preparation
• Scholarly/intellectual emphasis
• Academic effort/involvement
• Number of essay exams in courses
• Supportive relationships
• Quality of interactions with students
• Cumulative credit hours taken
• Extracurricular involvement
• Integration of ideas
• Course challenge/effort
• Coursework ratio of liberal arts courses to vocational/technical courses

Variable: Liberal Arts Emphasis II (Institutional Level)
  (alpha reliability = .78)
All scales and items in the Liberal Arts Emphasis I variable plus:
• Number of courses required of all students
• Percent of enrolled students living on campus
• Percent of student body who are undergraduates

Variable: Liberal Arts Experiences (Individual Level)
  (alpha reliability = .78)
All items in the Liberal Arts Emphasis I scale but at the individual student level rather than the institutional aggregate level

[a]Detailed operational definitions of all constituent scales and items are shown in Appendix A.

colleges and universities: the number of courses required of all students, the percent of students living on campus, and the percent of the total student body that was undergraduates. In developing both operational definitions of an institution's liberal arts emphasis, all constituent items were standardized and summed for each student. Thus, each constituent item counted equally in the computation of the total score. An institution's score was the average of students' scores on the liberal arts emphasis variable at that specific institution. This score was then assigned to each individual student in the study.

A third variant of the liberal arts emphasis variable was termed *liberal arts experiences*. The liberal arts experiences variable (LAEXP) was an individual-level variable based on the composite of an individual student's scores on the fourteen scales and items shown in Part A of Exhibit 2. This independent variable was summed across the first, second, or third years of the study, depending on the dependent variable predicted.

Because the liberal arts emphasis and liberal arts experience scales were intended to measure an orientation toward liberal arts education, it was expected that they would be characteristic of liberal arts colleges. Consequently, to estimate the construct validity of the scales, we regressed them on attendance at a liberal arts college (versus other institutional types), with controls introduced for students' precollege characteristics. In all three analyses, the liberal arts emphasis and experience scales strongly differentiated liberal arts colleges from other types of institutions. Liberal arts colleges had net advantages over research universities of 2.37 standard deviations on the LAEMP I scale, 2.45 standard deviations on the LAEMP II scale, and .68 of a standard deviation on the LAEXP scale. The corresponding advantages for liberal arts colleges over regional institutions were 1.79 standard deviations, 2.01 standard deviations, and .51 of a standard deviation, respectively.

To estimate the net effects of an institution's liberal arts emphasis and students' liberal arts experiences on intellectual and personal development during college, analyses of the NSSL data were carried out in three stages. In the first stage, each NSSL measure of intellectual and personal development was regressed on the liberal arts emphasis or liberal arts experience variable and all the control variables shown in Part B of Appendix B, except the measure of the average tested academic ability (or selectivity) of an institution's student body. In the second stage of the analyses, institutional selectivity and the categorical variables representing institutional type (that is, liberal arts colleges versus other institutions) were added to the first stage regression models. The results of these analyses permitted us to determine whether an institution's liberal arts emphasis or students' liberal arts experiences influenced developmental outcomes that were independent not only of students' characteristics but also of institutional selectivity and institutional type. The third stage of the analyses tested for the presence of conditional effects, considering students' background characteristics such as sex, race, precollege scores on each measure of intellectual and personal development, and the like.

Results

The statistically significant estimated effects of an institution's liberal arts emphasis and individual students' liberal arts experiences are summarized in Table 5. The first three columns show estimated effects controlling for students' precollege characteristics, while columns 4 through 6 show effects controlling not only for precollege characteristics but also for institutional selectivity and institutional type (that is, liberal arts colleges, research universities, and regional institutions). Because the three independent variables (LAEMP I, LAEMP II, and LAEXP) are continuous rather than categorical, the numbers shown in Table 5 are standardized (Beta) coefficients. These coefficients represent that part of a standard deviation increase in the outcome linked to one standard deviation increase in the independent variable, statistically controlling for all other influences in the regression equation. The only exception was when a plan to obtain a graduate degree was the outcome variable. Because it was a categorical variable, the coefficients in Table 5 for graduate degree plans represent the net increase in the odds of planning a graduate degree for every one unit increase in the independent variable.

Liberal Arts Emphasis I

An institution's LAEMP I was its average score on a composite of fourteen student first-year experiences. The experiences included such factors as quality of nonclassroom interactions with faculty, quality of teaching received, scholarly

TABLE 5
Statistically Significant Effects of an Institution's Liberal Arts Emphasis and Students' Liberal Arts Experiences on Intellectual and Personal Development (NSSL Data)[a]

Outcome	Controlling for Precollege Characteristics[b]			Controlling for Precollege Characteristics, College Selectivity, and College Type[c]		
	1	*2*	*3*	*4*	*5*	*6*
	LAEMP I	*LAEMP II*	*LAEXP*	*LAEMP I*	*LAEMP II*	*LAEXP*
Part A: First Year of College						
Reading comprehension	.068	.065	.050	.081	.072	.045
Critical thinking	.058	.051	.067	.062		.062
Plans to obtain a graduate degree		1.050				1.050
Openness to diversity/challenge	.069	.090	.180			.169
Learning for self-understanding		.086	.125			.109
Internal locus of attribution for academic success			.096			.103
Preference for higher-order cognitive activities	.045		.134			.131
Positive attitude toward literacy	.148					.155
Part B: Second Year of College						
Writing skills	.055	.057	.114	.141	.193	.117
Science reasoning					.102	.035
Plans to obtain a graduate degree			1.022			1.023
Openness to diversity/challenge	.121	.139	.173	.072	.162	.155
Internal locus of attribution for academic success			.130			.136
Preference for higher-order cognitive activities	.075	.073	.207			.204
Positive attitude toward literacy		.045	.242			.247

(Continued)

TABLE 5

Statistically Significant Effects of an Institution's Liberal Arts Emphasis and Students' Liberal Arts Experiences on Intellectual and Personal Development (NSSL Data)[a] (Continued)

Outcome	Controlling for Precollege Characteristics[b]			Controlling for Precollege Characteristics, College Selectivity, and College Type[c]		
	1 LAEMP I	2 LAEMP II	3 LAEXP	4 LAEMP I	5 LAEMP II	6 LAEXP
Part C: Third Year of College						
Reading comprehension	.049	.050	.125	.083	.117	.127
Critical thinking			.086			.086
Plans to obtain a graduate degree			1.012			1.016
Openness to diversity/challenge	.085	.087	.242			.230
Learning for self-understanding	.128	.132	.198			.159
Internal locus of attribution for academic success			.132			.152
Preference for higher-order cognitive activities			.197			.202
Positive attitude toward literacy			.235			.241

[a]All coefficients shown are standardized (Beta) weights, indicating that part of a standard deviation increase in the outcome associated with one standard deviation increase in the independent variable, controlling for all other variables indicated in notes *b* or *c*.

[b]Equations include controls for tested precollege academic ability (composite of CAAP reading comprehension, mathematics, and critical thinking) or a parallel pretest for reading comprehension, mathematics, or critical thinking; precollege plans to obtain a graduate degree; precollege academic motivation; college attended was first choice; age; sex; race; parents' education; parents' income; secondary school grades; time spent during high school working for pay; a scale consisting of time spent during high school in seven activities (studying, socializing with friends, talking with teachers outside class, exercising or sports, studying with friends, volunteer work, and extracurricular activities); and an exact parallel precollege measure of all other outcomes.

[c]Equations include all controls shown in note *b* plus college selectivity (composite of CAAP reading comprehension, mathematics, and critical thinking) of students at the institution attended, and dummy variables for college type (liberal arts colleges, research universities, and regional institutions).

and intellectual emphasis, integration of ideas, quality of interactions with peers, ratio of liberal arts courses to vocational technical courses, and the like. Column 1 in Table 5 summarizes the effects of an institution's LAEMP I score controlling for students' precollege characteristics, while column 4 summarizes the corresponding effects with controls for institutional selectivity and type in addition to students' precollege characteristics. Net of students' precollege characteristics, an institution's LAEMP I score had significant positive estimated impacts on the following outcomes:

- First- and third-year reading comprehension
- First-year critical thinking
- Second-year writing skills
- First-, second-, and third-year openness to diversity
- Third-year learning for self-understanding
- First- and second-year preference for higher-order cognitive tasks
- First-year positive attitude toward literacy.

With additional statistical controls in place for institutional selectivity and institutional type, most of the significant effects of an institution's LAEMP I score on measures of students' psychosocial or attitudinal development became nonsignificant. The only exception was a significant positive effect on second-year openness to diversity and challenge. The positive impacts of an institution's LAEMP I score on measures of intellectual and cognitive growth (that is, first- and third-year reading comprehension, first-year critical thinking, and second-year writing skills) remained significant, however, and increased in magnitude when institutional selectivity and type were taken into account.

Liberal Arts Emphasis II

An institution's LAEMP II was its average score on the composite of fourteen student first-year experiences that LAEMP I comprised plus three additional institutional characteristics: number of courses required of all students, percent of students living on campus, and percent of the student body who were undergraduates. Because the LAEMP II variable is so similar to the LAEMP I variable, it is not particularly surprising that, with some exceptions, it had essentially the same effects on measures of intellectual and personal growth during college (see columns 2 and 5 of Table 5). Across all three years of the study, the effects of the two institutional-level variables differed on only five of eighteen dimensions. Net of students' precollege characteristics, an institution's LAEMP II score had significant positive effects on first-year learning for self-understanding and plans for a graduate degree and second-year positive attitude toward literacy. The corresponding effects for the LAEMP I variable were nonsignificant. Conversely, the LAEMP II variable had only chance effects on growth in two outcomes that were positively influenced by an institution's LAEMP I score: first-year preference for higher-order cognitive tasks and positive attitude toward literacy. With additional controls for institutional selectivity and type, a college's LAEMP II score had significant positive effects on second-year science reasoning but not on first-year critical thinking. Conversely, an institution's LAEMP I variable had a non-significant influence on science reasoning but a positive impact on first-year critical thinking.

Liberal Arts Experiences

A student's LAEXP score was an individual-level composite of his or her scores on the fourteen items and scales constituting the LAEMP I variable. The LAEXP score was aggregated across the first, second, or third year of college, depending on the measure of intellectual or personal development predicted. Column 3 in Table 5 summarizes the effects of a student's LAEXP score controlling for students' precollege characteristics, while column 6 summarizes the corresponding effects with controls for institutional selectivity and type in addition to students' precollege characteristics. Net of students' precollege characteristics, a student's LAEXP score had significant positive estimated impacts on the following measures:

- First- and third-year reading comprehension and critical thinking
- Second-year writing skills
- Second- and third-year plans to obtain a graduate degree

- First-, second-, and third-year openness to diversity, internal locus of attribution for academic success, and preference for higher-order cognitive activities
- First- and third-year learning for self-understanding
- Second- and third-year positive attitude toward literacy.

With additional statistical controls for institutional selectivity and institutional type, a student's LAEXP score had significant positive effects, not only on each of the above outcomes but also on first-year plans to obtain a graduate degree, first-year positive attitude toward literacy, and second-year science reasoning.

Timing of Impacts

Like the estimated effect of attendance at a liberal arts college (versus another type of institution), there is little in the evidence summarized in Table 5 to suggest that the impacts of an institution's liberal arts education emphasis increases appreciably in scope or magnitude subsequent to the initial year of college. This situation was clearly not the case with students' liberal arts experiences, however. Looking at just those estimated effects summarized in column 6 of Table 5, it is clear that from the first to the third year of college, the positive net influence of composite liberal arts experiences increased in magnitude. For example, comparing the first to the third year of college, the net effect of the LAEXP score increased from .045 to .127 for reading comprehension, .062 to .086 for critical thinking, .169 to .230 for openness to diversity, .109 to .159 for learning for self-understanding, .103 to .152 for internal locus of attribution, .131 to .202 for preference for higher-order cognitive tasks, and .155 to .241 for positive attitude toward literacy. The only outcome where this trend did not hold was plans for a graduate degree, where the positive effect of students' liberal arts experiences diminished slightly from the first to the third year of college.

Despite these increases in the magnitude of the impact of students' liberal arts experiences from the first to the third year of college, the largest incremental impacts still appeared to occur in the initial year of exposure to postsecondary education. The median first-year effect size was about 68 percent of the median third-year effect size.

Conditional Effects

Although the evidence in the previous chapter indicates that the estimated effects of attending a liberal arts college (versus another type of institution) on growth in intellectual and personal development during college tended to be general rather than conditional, it was not the case with an institution's liberal arts emphasis or student's liberal arts experiences. Our analyses indicated that both measures of an institution's liberal arts emphasis as well as students' liberal arts experiences had statistically significant conditional effects based on race, sex, and a student's precollege score on several of the intellectual and personal outcomes considered. Thus, although Table 5 shows the average net effects of an institution's liberal arts emphasis and students' liberal arts experiences, independent of race, sex, and students' precollege characteristics, the presence of significant conditional effects suggests that some of these effects may actually vary in magnitude by sex, race, and students' precollege scores on an outcome. The nature of these conditional effects is summarized in Exhibit 3. As Parts A and B of the exhibit indicate, eight conditional effects involved students' precollege scores on end-of-first, second- or third-year measures of intellectual and personal development. On six of those conditional effects (first- and third-year reading comprehension; first-year internal locus of attribution for academic success; and second-year writing skills, science reasoning, and graduate degree plans), the influence of an institution's liberal arts emphasis and students' liberal arts experiences acted in a compensatory manner. That is, the positive influence of an institution's liberal arts emphasis or students' liberal arts experiences on each of these six outcomes was significantly stronger for students who began college with initially low scores on the outcome than for their counterparts who entered college with initially high scores on the outcome.

Although the weight of evidence suggested that a school's liberal arts emphasis or students' liberal arts experiences function as a compensatory influence on intellectual and personal growth during college, there was an exception

EXHIBIT 3
Significant Estimated Conditional Effects of an Institution's Liberal Arts Emphasis (LAEMP I or II) or Students' Liberal Arts Experiences (LAEXP) (NSSL Data)

Part A   Outcomes on which the net positive effects of an institution's liberal arts emphasis or students' liberal arts experiences were statistically significant for students below the mean on the precollege measure of the outcome, and significantly more positive for students below the precollege mean than for students above the precollege mean:

• End-of-first-year reading comprehension (LAEMP II)
• End-of-first-year internal locus of attribution for academic success (LAEMP I)
• End-of-second-year writing skills (LAEMP I and II)
• End-of-second-year science reasoning (LAEXP)
• End-of-second-year plans to obtain a graduate degree (LAEXP)
• End-of-third-year reading comprehension (LAEXP)

Part B   Outcomes on which the net positive effects of students' liberal arts experiences were statistically significant for students above the mean on the precollege measure of the outcome, and significantly more positive for students above the precollege mean than for students below the precollege mean:

• End-of-second-year positive attitude toward literacy (LAEXP)
• End-of-third-year positive attitude toward literacy (LAEXP)

Part C Outcomes on which the net positive effects of an institution's liberal arts emphasis or students' liberal arts experiences were statistically significant for students of color, and significantly more positive for students of color than for white students:

• End-of-first-year reading comprehension (LAEMP II)
• End-of-second-year science reasoning (LAEXP)
• End-of-third-year reading comprehension (LAEMP II)

Part D   Outcomes on which the net positive effects of students' liberal arts experiences were statistically significant for white students, and significantly more positive for white students than for students of color:

• End-of-second-year graduate degree plans (LAEXP)

Part E   Outcomes on which the net positive effects of an institution's liberal arts emphasis or students' liberal arts experiences were statistically significant for women, and significantly more positive for women than for men:

• End-of-first-year positive attitude toward literacy (LAEMP I)
• End-of-second-year writing skills (LAEMP I and II, LAEXP)

to this trend. The impact of students' liberal arts experiences on second- and third-year positive attitude toward literacy tended to act in a manner that accentuated precollege differences on this dimension. That is, liberal arts experiences had a significantly stronger positive impact on attitude toward literacy for students who were initially high scorers on this dimension when they entered college than for their peers who began college with relatively less positive attitudes toward literacy.

Evidence also suggested, as summarized in Part C of Exhibit 3, that an institution's liberal arts emphasis and students' liberal arts experiences had stronger positive impacts on such cognitively oriented outcomes as reading comprehension and science reasoning for students of color than for their white peers. Conversely, students' liberal arts experiences were significantly more likely to enhance the graduate degree plans of white students than students of color (Part D).

Finally, a modicum of evidence indicated that the impact of an institution's liberal arts emphasis on some dimensions of intellectual and personal growth during college may be more salient for women than for men. As indicated in Part E of Exhibit 3, an institution's liberal arts emphasis had stronger positive effects on both literacy attitudes and writing skills for female students than for their male counterparts.

Long-Term Effects of Liberal Arts Colleges

T O ESTIMATE THE LONG-TERM IMPACT of liberal arts colleges, we analyzed data from the Appalachian College Association study. These data followed samples of alumni from private baccalaureate-level liberal arts colleges, public regional universities, and private master's level institutions located in four states in the Appalachian region for five, fifteen, and twenty-five years after their graduation from college.

Data and Analyses

The richness of the ACA study data permitted us to estimate the net effects of attending a baccalaureate liberal arts college on an extensive range of measures of graduates' personal and professional lives as well as their retrospective perceptions of the impact of their undergraduate education. These various outcomes are listed in Exhibit 4. As the exhibit indicates, the outcomes include graduate degree attainment and graduate degree plans for children; retrospective perceptions of the impact of one's undergraduate college and overall satisfaction with the undergraduate experience; labor market experiences; community, social, and political involvement; savings behavior and charitable donations; involvement in continuing education; health status and health-related behaviors; satisfaction with life and sense of control over life events; region of the country in which one lives and works; and the importance of different skills and values in one's current endeavors. More detailed operational definitions of all long-term outcomes, including applicable scale reliabilities, are shown in Part C of Appendix A.

EXHIBIT 4
Long-Term Outcomes of College Assessed by the Study
(ACA Study Data)[a]

Current graduate degree attainment
Current graduate degree goal
Graduate degree goal for dependent children
Retrospective perceptions of undergraduate college's impact on:
    Learning and intellectual development
    Development of leadership/self-efficacy skills
    Personal and spiritual development
    Responsible citizenship
    Development of scientific/quantitative skills
Overall satisfaction with the undergraduate experience
Currently employed full time
Employed in a for-profit business or organization
Extent to which undergraduate experiences prepared one for:
    First job
    Current job
Annual salary
Annual household income
Satisfaction with one's job:
    Autonomy
    Personal fulfillment
    Financial characteristics
Community and social involvement
Religious involvement
Voting behavior:
    Local elections
    State elections
    National elections
Run for political office
Appointed to political office
Elected to political office
Campaigned for someone running for political office
Percentage of income saved
Percentage of income donated to charity
Number of continuing education courses taken for:
    Career/professional advancement
    Personal development

EXHIBIT 4 (Continued)

Current health status
Frequency of alcoholic beverage consumption
Frequency of cigarette smoking
Frequency of aerobic exercise
Sense of control over life events
Satisfaction with life
Currently live in the Appalachian region
Currently work in the Appalachian region
Years living in the Appalachian region
Years working in the Appalachian region
Importance in one's current endeavor of:
    Learning and intellectual development
    Leadership/self-efficacy skills
    Personal and spiritual development
    Responsible citizenship
    Scientific/quantitative skills

[a]Detailed operational definitions of all variables are shown in Appendix A (Part C).

Our analyses of the ACA data were carried out in three stages. In the first stage, we regressed each long-term outcome in the ACA data shown in Exhibit 5 on the categorical variables representing graduation from a baccalaureate liberal arts college (versus another type of institution) and all the "basic controls" shown in Part C of Appendix B (that is, student background/demographic characteristics, precollege ACT scores, college graduation cohort, and a measure of institutional selectivity). This regression model provided an estimate of the total effect of attending a liberal arts college on each outcome. In the second stage of the analyses, we added appropriate additional controls to the first stage regression model (see "additional controls" in Part C of Appendix B). Doing so allowed us to determine how much of the total effect of attending a liberal arts college was mediated or explained by distinctive undergraduate experiences and distinctive intervening life experiences and attainments. In the third stage of the analyses, we tested for the presence of conditional effects, considering variables such as sex, race, precollege ACT scores, and graduation cohort.

Results: Total and Direct Effects

Our estimates of the total and direct effects of attending a baccalaureate liberal arts college (versus a public regional university or a private master's-granting institution) on retrospective perceptions of college impact, labor market outcomes, and personal life outcomes are summarized in Table 6. Part A of the table shows the significant total and direct effects of attending a baccalaureate liberal arts college (versus a comparison institution) on graduates' retrospective perceptions of the impact of their undergraduate education. As Part A of Table 6 shows, alumni of liberal arts colleges reported significantly greater impact than their counterparts who graduated from public regional institutions but a general parity with alumni of private master's institutions. Net of a battery of statistical controls that included ACT scores, secondary school grades, family background, graduation cohort, and institutional selectivity, alumni of baccalaureate liberal arts colleges reported that their undergraduate experience had a significantly stronger positive impact on their learning and intellectual development, the development of leadership and self-efficacy skills, personal and spiritual development, and the development of responsible citizenship than did similar graduates of public universities. Baccalaureate liberal arts college alumni also indicated significantly greater satisfaction with their undergraduate education than did public regional university graduates. These significant effects persisted even when additional controls were introduced for college grades, loan debt accumulated during college, and level of current educational degree attained.

The magnitude of the statistically significant effects was modest, ranging from .15 to .61 of a standard deviation, with a median value of about .25 of a standard deviation. Net of other factors, baccalaureate liberal arts colleges had only chance total and direct impacts on the development of scientific and quantitative skills.

Part B of Table 6 summarizes the estimated significant effects of attending a baccalaureate liberal arts college on labor market outcomes. Labor market outcomes included graduate degree attainment, because attainment of a graduate or professional degree is a major determinant of success in the labor market. As the table indicates, the effects of attending a baccalaureate liberal arts college were mixed. Net of other factors, including precollege degree aspirations, liberal arts college alumni were about 1.27 times as likely to obtain a graduate or professional degree as graduates of public institutions. It did not automatically translate into income-related labor market advantages, however. Compared with similar graduates of public universities, alumni of baccalaureate liberal arts colleges were significantly less likely to be employed full time and to be employed in a for-profit business or organization than public regional university graduates. Similarly, liberal arts college graduates had a small but statistically significant disadvantage in annual salary relative to public university alumni. This negative total effect, however, was in all likelihood attributable to differences in undergraduate major field of study and differential rates of employment in for-profit businesses or organizations between graduates of liberal arts colleges and public universities. The earnings disadvantage became nonsignificant when these differences were taken into account.

Conversely, graduation from a baccalaureate liberal arts college was also linked to a number of positive effects on labor market outcomes. Net of all other influences, including academic major and sector of employment, alumni of baccalaureate liberal arts colleges had small but statistically significant advantages over graduates of master's level private colleges in both annual salary and household income. Similarly, liberal arts college graduates also were significantly more likely than public university graduates to report that their undergraduate experiences prepared them adequately for both their first and current job. When differences in such factors as academic major, college grades, and perceptions of college impact were taken into account, however, these positive total effects became nonsignificant, suggesting that the positive influence of liberal arts colleges on career preparation is largely attributable to differences in the undergraduate experience associated with attendance at a baccalaureate liberal arts college versus a public regional university.

The statistically significant positive and negative effects of liberal arts colleges on career preparation, earnings, and income were quite modest in magnitude. They ranged in absolute size from about .11 to .19 of a standard deviation, with a median value of only .11 of a standard deviation. No evidence indicated that liberal arts college graduates were more or less satisfied with the autonomy, personal fulfillment, or financial characteristics of their jobs than were graduates of other types of institutions.

TABLE 6
Significant Estimated Effects of Attending a Baccalaureate Liberal Arts College (versus a Public Regional University or a Private Master's Institution) on College Impact, Labor Market Outcomes, and Personal Life Outcomes[a]

Outcome	Baccalaureate Liberal Arts Colleges versus Public Regional Universities			Baccalaureate Liberal Arts Colleges versus Private Master's Institution		
	B^j	Effect Size[k]	Odds Ratio[l]	B^j	Effect Size[k]	Odds Ratio[l]
Part A: Undergraduate College Impact						
Undergraduate college's impact on:						
Learning and intellectual development						
(Total Effect)[b]	1.135	.248				
(Direct Effect)[c]	1.046	.228				
Development of leadership/self-efficacy skills						
(Total Effect)[b]	1.018	.155				
(Direct Effect)[c]	.954	.146				
Personal and spiritual development						
(Total Effect)[b]	2.666	.610				
(Direct Effect)[c]	2.637	.603				
Responsible citizenship						
(Total Effect)[b]	.858	.273				
(Direct Effect)[c]	.874	.279				
Overall satisfaction with undergraduate education						
(Total Effect)[b]	.178	.234				
(Direct Effect)[c]	.167	.219				
Part B: Labor Market Outcomes						
Current graduate degree attainment						
(Direct Effect)[b]	.237					1.27

Employed full-time				
(Total Effect)[b]	-.297			0.74
(Direct Effect)[d]	-.322			0.73
Employed in a for-profit business or organization				
(Total Effect)[b]	-.344			0.71
(Direct Effect)[d]	-.331			0.72
Extent to which undergraduate experience prepared one for first job				
(Total Effect)[b]	.118	.107		
Extent to which undergraduate experiences prepared one for current job				
(Total Effect)[b]	.209	.186		
Annual Salary				
(Total Effect)[b]	-.218	-.114		
(Direct Effect)[e]			.205	.107
Household income				
(Total Effect)[e]			.264	.144
Part C: Personal Life Outcomes				
Religious involvement				
(Total Effect)[b]	.316	.304	.109	.105
(Direct Effect)[f]	.168	.162	.125	.120
Percentage of income donated to charity				
(Total Effect)[b]	.177	.196		
Frequency of voting in national election				
(Direct Effect)[f]	-.123	-.135		
Campaigned for, or assisted someone running for political office				
(Direct Effect)[f]	-.264			0.77

(Continued)

TABLE 6
Significant Estimated Effects of Attending a Baccalaureate Liberal Arts College (versus a Public Regional University or a Private Master's Institution) on College Impact, Labor Market Outcomes, and Personal Life Outcomes[a] (Continued)

Outcome	Baccalaureate Liberal Arts Colleges versus Public Regional Universities			Baccalaureate Liberal Arts Colleges versus Private Master's Institution		
	B^j	Effect Size[k]	Odds Ratio[l]	B^j	Effect Size[k]	Odds Ratio[l]
Number of continuing education courses taken for personal development (Total Effect)[b]	.101	.103				
Frequency of alcoholic beverage consumption (Total Effect)[g]	−.164	−.252				
(Direct Effect)[h]	−.133	−.205				
Frequency of cigarette smoking (Direct Effect)[h]				−.046	−.088	
Currently working in the Appalachian region (Direct Effect)[i]	.207		1.23	.285		1.33
Years living in the Appalachian region (Direct Effect)[i]				.127	.083	
Years working in the Appalachian region (Direct Effect)[i]				.105	.070	
Importance in one's current endeavors of: Learning and intellectual development (Total Effect)[b]	.642	.146		.450	.103	

Personal and spiritual development

(Total Effect)[b]   .910   .224

Responsible citizenship

(Total Effect)[b]   .406   .135

[a]No significant net effects of baccalaureate liberal arts colleges were found for the following outcomes: current graduate degree goal; graduate degree goal for children; undergraduate college influence on scientific and quantitative skills; satisfaction with autonomy; personal fulfillment, or financial characteristics of job; community and social involvement; percentage of income saved; voting in local or state elections; running for political office; being appointed or elected to political office; continuing education courses taken for career/professional advancement; current health status; frequency of aerobic exercise; sense of control over life events; satisfaction with life; currently living in the Appalachian region; and importance in one's current endeavors of leadership/self-efficacy skills and scientific/quantitative skills.

[b]Equations also include *basic controls* (ACT composite score, precollege graduate degree plans, precollege graduate degree goals, secondary school grades, age, race, sex, parents' educational attainment, parents' income, college attended was first choice, precollege expectations to apply for financial aid, dummy variables representing graduation cohort [1974–76, 1984–86, 1994–96, lived in the Appalachian region when graduating from high school, and the academic selectivity of the institution attended [average ACT composite of students]).

[c]Equations also include *basic controls*, college grades, loan debt, and educational attainment.

[d]Equations also include *basic controls*, college grades, educational attainment, dummy variables for college major, five retrospective college impact scores, and marital status.

[e]Equations also include *basic controls*, college grades, educational attainment, marital status, dummy variables for college major, five retrospective college impact scores, working in the Appalachian region, and employed in a for-profit business or organization. Additional controls for annual salary include actual and perceived congruence between current job and academic major.

[f]Equations also include *basic controls*, college grades, educational attainment, marital status, dummy variables for college majors, five retrospective college impact scores, full-time employment, household income, and currently living in the Appalachian region.

[g]Equations also include *basic controls* and self-rated health status in college.

[h]Equations also include *basic controls*, self-rated health status in college, college grades, educational attainment, marital status, dummy variables for college major, five retrospective college impact scores, full-time employment, household income, and currently being in the Appalachian region.

[i]Equations also include *basic controls*, college grades, educational attainment, marital status, dummy variables for college major, five retrospective college impact scores, full-time employment, and household income.

[j]The unstandardized regression coefficient (B) is the average statistically adjusted difference between baccalaureate liberal arts college alumni and comparison institution alumni on the dependent variable. A positive sign means that baccalaureate liberal arts college alumni have a higher adjusted score on the variables, while a negative sign means they have a lower adjusted score on the variable.

[k]*Effect size* is used when the dependent variable is continuous. It is computed by dividing the regression coefficient by the pooled standard deviation of the dependent variable and indicates that fraction of a standard deviation that baccalaureate liberal arts college alumni are advantaged or disadvantaged (depending on the sign) relative to the comparison institution alumni.

[l]*Odds ratio* is used when the dependent variable is dichotomous (yes or no). It indicates the odds of baccalaureate liberal arts college alumni indicating "yes" versus the comparison institution alumni.

Part C of Table 6 summarizes the significant estimate effects of baccalaureate liberal arts colleges on personal life outcomes. Although baccalaureate liberal arts college alumni did not have higher levels of community or social involvement, they did report higher levels of religious involvement than did alumni of both public universities and private master's institutions. This finding may reflect the religious affiliation of many of the baccalaureate liberal arts colleges in our sample; it is not clear whether this finding reflects a socializing effect of one's undergraduate experience or merely the fact that the baccalaureate liberal arts institutions tended to recruit and enroll students with pronounced levels of religious involvement before college.

No evidence indicated that alumni of baccalaureate liberal arts colleges saved a greater percentage of their income or took more continuing education courses for career advancement than did alumni of comparison institutions. Compared with graduates of public universities, however, liberal arts college graduates donated a significantly greater percentage of their income to charity and took significantly more continuing education courses for personal development. Because these latter two effects were not significant when college experience variables such as major, grades, and dimensions of college impact were taken into account, it suggests that they may be explained in part by differences in the undergraduate experiences at baccalaureate liberal arts colleges and public universities.

On most dimensions of political involvement (that is, voting in local or state elections, running for political office, and being appointed or elected to political office), only chance net differences existed between alumni of baccalaureate liberal arts colleges and their counterparts from other types of institutions. Irrespective of other influences, however, liberal arts college graduates were modestly less likely than alumni of public universities to vote in national elections or to participate in a candidate's political campaign.

Controlling for a battery of potential confounding influences, including health status in college, graduating from a baccalaureate liberal arts college had only chance effects on current health status and frequency of aerobic exercise. On two other health-related behaviors, however, liberal arts college alumni differed modestly from their counterparts graduating from other types of institutions. Net of precollege characteristics, college experiences, and postgraduation labor market experiences, liberal arts college graduates had significantly lower levels of alcohol consumption than alumni of public universities and significantly lower levels of cigarette smoking than alumni of private master's level institutions. No significant net differences were found between baccalaureate liberal arts college alumni and graduates of other types of institutions in sense of control over life events or satisfaction with life.

Our analyses uncovered no statistically significant evidence to indicate that baccalaureate liberal arts college alumni were any more likely than alumni from other types of institutions to be currently living in the Appalachian region (that is, the region where they attended college). This finding was not the case, however, for whether or not one was currently working in the Appalachian region or for the years one lived and worked in the Appalachian region. Net of an extensive battery of precollege variables, college experiences, and labor market experiences, including graduation cohort, age, and whether or not one lived in the Appalachian region before college, liberal arts college alumni were 1.23 times as likely to be currently working in the Appalachian region as graduates of public universities and 1.33 times as likely to be currently working in Appalachia as alumni of private master's level institutions. With the same set of statistical controls in effect, baccalaureate liberal arts college graduates indicated a small but statistically significant advantage over alumni of private master's institutions in both the years they had lived and the years they had worked in the Appalachian region.

Finally, we uncovered statistically reliable evidence to suggest that the dimensions that were uniquely influenced by an undergraduate liberal arts education persisted in the current lives of graduates. Net of precollege characteristics, graduation cohort, and institutional selectivity, baccalaureate liberal arts college alumni reported that learning and intellectual development were modestly but significantly more important in their current lives than did alumni of either public universities or private master's level institutions. Similarly, in the presence of the same battery of statistical controls, liberal arts college graduates indicated that both personal and spiritual development and responsible citizenship were more important in their current lives than did graduates of public universities. In all cases, these positive total effects became nonsignificant when measures of college experiences and postcollege lives were added to the prediction equations. Such evidence suggests that the positive total effects on these outcomes are largely explained by the unique college experiences and postcollege lives of liberal arts college graduates.

Results: Conditional Effects

Our analyses to determine the presence of conditional long-term effects of graduating from a baccalaureate liberal arts college were statistically significant for sex, precollege ACT scores, and graduation cohort. The nature of these conditional effects is summarized in Exhibit 5.

Part A of Exhibit 5 summarizes the conditional effects by sex. For five outcomes, the net positive impact of attending a baccalaureate liberal arts college (versus another type of institution) was significantly larger in magnitude for male than for female graduates. In the general effects results (based on the aggregate or combined sample) discussed previously, we saw that alumni of liberal arts colleges had advantages relative to alumni of public regional institutions in graduate degree attainment, overall satisfaction with college, and percent of income donated to charity. Our analysis of conditional effects, however, indicated that these advantages were significantly more pronounced for male than for female graduates. Moreover, in the aggregate sample and in terms of satisfaction with college, percent of income donated to charity, and number of continuing education courses taken for personal development, the chance differences between alumni of liberal arts colleges and private master's institutions masked a distinct advantage among male graduates of baccalaureate liberal arts colleges relative to male graduates of private master's institutions. Similarly, in the aggregate sample, only chance differences were uncovered between baccalaureate liberal arts college graduates and alumni of other types of institutions in lifetime graduate degree goals. Again, this aggregate finding masked a conditional effect in which male graduates of liberal arts colleges had significantly higher graduate degree goals than male graduates of either public regional universities or private master's-level institutions.

Part B of Exhibit 5 summarizes the significant conditional effects involving precollege ACT scores. On five of the outcomes we considered, the net positive impacts of graduating from a baccalaureate liberal arts college were

EXHIBIT 5
Significant Estimated Conditional Effects of Baccalaureate Liberal Arts Colleges (versus Public Regional Universities and Private Master's Institutions) (ACA Data)

Part A
Outcomes on which the net positive effects of attending a baccalaureate liberal arts college (versus another type of institution) were statistically significant for men, and significantly more positive for men than women:
• Current graduate degree attainment (versus public regional universities [PRU])
• Current lifetime graduate degree goal (versus both PRU and private master's institutions [PMI])
• Overall satisfaction with college (versus both PRU and PMI)
• Percentage of income donated to charity (versus both PRU and PMI)
• Number of continuing education courses taken for personal development (versus PRU)

Part B
Outcomes on which the net positive effects of attending a baccalaureate liberal arts college (versus another type of institution) were statistically significant for alumni with ACT scores below the sample mean, and significantly more positive for alumni with ACT scores below the sample mean than for alumni with ACT scores above the mean:
• Annual salary (versus PMI)
• Currently live in the Appalachian region (versus PRU)
• Currently work in the Appalachian region (versus PRU)
• Years living in the Appalachian region (versus both PRU and PMI)
• Years working in the Appalachian region (versus PRU)

Part C
Outcomes on which the net positive effects of attending a baccalaureate liberal arts college (versus another type of institution) were statistically significant for older alumni (1974–76 graduates), and significantly more positive for older alumni than for more recent graduates (1994–96 graduates):
• Graduate degree goal for children (versus PMI)
• Undergraduate college's impact on personal and spiritual development (versus PRU)
• Currently live in the Appalachian region (versus both PRU and PMI)
• Years living in the Appalachian region (versus PMI)
• Years working in the Appalachian region (versus PMI)

Part D
Outcomes on which the net positive effects of attending a baccalaureate liberal arts college (versus another type of institution) were statistically significant for more recent alumni (1994–96 graduates), and significantly more positive for more recent alumni than for older alumni (1974–76 graduates):
• Undergraduate college's impact on the development of responsible citizenship (versus both PRU and PMI)
• Undergraduate college's impact on the development of scientific/quantitative skills (versus PMI)

significantly more pronounced for alumni who began postsecondary education with relatively low tested academic preparation than for alumni who entered college with relatively high levels of tested academic preparation. In the aggregate sample, graduates of liberal arts colleges earned higher salaries and spent more years living in the Appalachian region than alumni of private master's level institutions. They were also more likely to be currently working in Appalachia than public university graduates. On all three outcomes, however, the results based on the aggregate sample masked the fact that these positive effects of baccalaureate liberal arts colleges were significantly more pronounced for alumni with precollege ACT scores below the sample mean than for alumni with precollege ACT scores above the mean. Similarly, in the aggregate sample, no net differences were found between liberal arts college and public university alumni in the likelihood of currently living in the Appalachian region or the number of years they had lived or had worked in Appalachia. These nonsignificant differences in the overall sample, however, masked conditional effects in which graduates of liberal arts colleges with ACT scores below the mean demonstrated significantly greater net advantages on all three outcomes than graduates of public universities who entered college with similarly low levels of academic preparation.

Parts C and D of Exhibit 5 summarize the conditional effects involving graduation cohort. Part C lists the five outcomes on which the positive effects of attending a baccalaureate liberal arts college were significantly larger in magnitude for older alumni (1974–76 cohort than) for more recent graduates (1994–96 cohort). In the aggregate sample, graduates of liberal arts colleges reported greater personal and spiritual development as a result of their undergraduate experience than public university alumni. Irrespective of the year in which they graduated from college, liberal arts college graduates also reported more years living and working in Appalachia than graduates of private master's level institutions. On all three outcomes, however, the significant effect for the combined sample masked the tendency for these positive impacts of baccalaureate liberal arts colleges to be significantly more pronounced for alumni graduating in the 1974–76 cohort than for alumni graduating in the 1994–96 cohort. Similarly, in the aggregate sample, no significant net differences were found between alumni of liberal arts colleges and graduates of other types of institutions in graduate degree goals for children or the probability of currently living in Appalachia. Yet these chance effects in the combined sample masked significant effects for the 1974–76 graduation cohort. Within this older graduation cohort, alumni of liberal arts colleges had significantly higher degree goals for their children than alumni of private master's level institutions and were significantly more likely to be currently living in Appalachia than alumni of either master's level institutions or public universities.

Part D of Exhibit 5 lists the two outcomes on which the positive effects of attending a baccalaureate liberal arts college were significantly larger for more recent graduates (1994–96 cohort) than for older graduates (1974–76 cohort). In the aggregate or combined sample, liberal arts college alumni reported that their undergraduate experience had a significantly greater impact on the development of responsible citizenship than did public university alumni. This finding, however, masked a tendency for the net positive effect of liberal arts colleges to be more pronounced for 1994–96 graduates than for 1974–76 graduates. Moreover, in the aggregate sample, no net differences existed between liberal arts college graduates and graduates of private master's institutions in their perceptions of the impact of their undergraduate experience on the development of either responsible citizenship or scientific and quantitative skills. Yet on both these scales, liberal arts college alumni who graduated in the 1994–96 cohort rated their undergraduate experience as significantly more influential and positive than master's level institution alumni in the same cohort.

Impacts of Liberal Arts Colleges and Liberal Arts Education: A Summary

I N ANALYZING TWO LONGITUDINAL DATASETS, this investigation sought answers to the following questions about liberal arts colleges and liberal arts education:

1. To what extent do liberal arts colleges uniquely foster empirically validated good practices in undergraduate education?
2. What are the net impacts of liberal arts colleges, an institution's liberal arts emphasis, and students' liberal arts experiences on intellectual and personal growth during college?
3. What are the net long-term impacts of attending a liberal arts education on alumni?
4. Are the net impacts of liberal arts colleges or liberal arts education the same for all students, or do they differ in magnitude for different kinds of students?

This summary and our conclusions are organized around these major questions.

Good Practices

Our findings suggest two major conclusions. First, they provide consistent evidence that, compared with research universities and regional institutions, liberal arts colleges do, in fact, uniquely foster a broad range of empirically substantiated good practices in undergraduate education. On some dimensions of good practice, such as extracurricular involvement and other measures of influential interaction with student peers, the positive influence of liberal arts colleges was attributable to their residential, full-time student body. On a broad range of good practice dimensions, however, liberal arts colleges demonstrated positive effects that were independent of their residential, full-time character as well as their academic selectivity and the precollege abilities, involvements, and motivations of the students they enrolled. These good practice dimensions included student-faculty contact, active learning and time on task, high expectations, quality of teaching, and a supportive campus environment. Just how liberal arts colleges are able to bring these results about is not as clear from our data. We suggest, however, that they may be attributable to a combination of factors.

The first of these factors is institutional size. As indicated previously, the median enrollment in the liberal arts colleges in our sample was 1,707 (compared with a median student enrollment of 22,990 in the sample's research universities and 12,478 in the sample's regional institutions). As suggested by Chickering and Reisser (1993), simply by virtue of their relatively small size, liberal arts colleges present students with a more manageable social-psychological environment that invites greater levels of student engagement than do larger institutions. Interestingly, in our findings, the impact of small size did not manifest itself in a student's interactions with his or her peers. The effects of attending a liberal arts college on measures of influential interaction with other students tended to become nonsignificant when attending college full time and living on campus were taken into account. Rather, the small size of liberal arts colleges may have had a more pronounced enabling influence on the frequency, quality, and impact of a student's relationships with faculty. In both the first and second year of postsecondary education, liberal arts college students reported higher levels of faculty interest in teaching and student development and the quality of their nonclassroom interactions with faculty than did similar students at either research universities or regional institutions. Though limited to relationships with faculty, such evidence supports recent efforts such as learning communities and living-learning centers that attempt to create more effective academic subenvironments within large universities (Inkelas and Weisman, 2003; Tinto and Goodsell, 1994).

Clearly, small institutional size and the attendant likelihood of small classes might have important implications not only for shaping the nature of student-faculty relationships but also for the quality and impact of teaching that occurs in liberal arts colleges (Astin, 1999; Ludlow, 1996; Wachtel, 1998). It is likely, however, that small size accounts for only part of the impact. What may be of equal if not greater importance is an institutional ethos or culture that places a premium on effective teaching and high academic expectations. This ethos or culture may be most pervasive at selective liberal arts colleges, but the evidence from this study, though admittedly indirect, suggests that it may be characteristic of liberal arts colleges irrespective of their level of selectivity. Controlling for selectivity of the student body as well as for an extensive battery of other confounding influences, liberal arts colleges in our sample still demonstrated significant first-year advantages over both research universities and regional institutions on measures of effective teaching and high expectations such as instructional skill and clarity, instructional organization and preparation, instructional emphasis on cooperative learning, the instructor's use of higher-order questioning techniques, emphasis on higher-order examination questions, students' academic effort and involvement, the challenge of and effort required for a course, and number of assigned readings and written reports.

How a culture that values both innovative and effective teaching and high academic expectations is created at a liberal arts college is probably the result of a complex interweaving of mutually reinforcing influences. Certainly, liberal arts colleges are more likely than other four-year institutions to attract and hire faculty who, for both personal and professional reasons, value good teaching (Leslie, 2002). Furthermore, these initial values are probably accentuated even further by interaction with similarly oriented faculty already at the institution. High academic expectations may also be shaped at least in part by faculty recruitment and hiring practices. It is likely, however, that creating an institutional culture of high intellectual expectations is also promoted through purposeful administrative policies that support and reinforce a challenging undergraduate academic experience both in and out of the classroom. Our findings suggest that an academically selective student body may not be a necessary prerequisite for such an institutional culture at liberal arts colleges.

Finally, if student precollege traits, selective admissions, and a residential full-time student body do not fully explain why liberal arts colleges foster good practices in undergraduate education, it further reinforces the importance of institutional policies and programs aimed at narrowing the gap in students' experiences between liberal arts colleges and other types of institutions. Learning communities, living-learning centers, first-year seminars, and similar interventions may offer several viable approaches for accomplishing this outcome at larger institutions (Inkelas and Weisman, 2003; Tinto and Goodsell, 1994; Upcraft, Gardner, and Associates, 1989).

A second major conclusion was that the estimated positive effects of liberal arts colleges on good practices were the most numerous and pronounced in magnitude during the first year of postsecondary education. Thereafter, the incremental contribution of each additional year of attendance at a liberal arts college over previous years became progressively smaller in magnitude. Such evidence is quite consistent with the notion that many of the most powerful educating experiences of liberal arts colleges are a function of intense socialization processes that occur primarily during the first year of exposure to postsecondary education (Chickering and Reisser, 1993; Hagedorn and others, 1999; Heath, 1968)—which does not mean that liberal arts colleges are having only a trivial influence on good practices in undergraduate education subsequent to one's initial exposure to postsecondary education. Our regression specifications were designed to estimate the incremental impact on good practices attributable to each successive year of attendance at a liberal arts college. The diminishing returns relationships we uncovered, however, do not mean that the emphasis on good practices in undergraduate education at liberal arts colleges is any less salient in the second and third years of postsecondary education than it was in the first year. Rather, what our findings suggest is that liberal arts colleges have their most pronounced impact on good practices in undergraduate education in the initial year of college. Thereafter, liberal arts colleges continue to significantly promote good practices above and beyond their first-year impact, but their additional contributions in subsequent years become fewer in number and smaller in magnitude.

Intellectual and Personal Development

Although it is clear that liberal arts colleges fostered the conditions that tend to produce an influential undergraduate experience, the estimated net impacts of attendance at a liberal arts college on measures of intellectual and personal development were somewhat mixed. Of the eleven different measures of intellectual and personal growth considered in the investigation, liberal arts colleges had no significant influence on two measures (plans to obtain a graduate degree and internal locus of attribution for academic success), negative effects on two measures (mathematics and science reasoning), and mixed effects on two measures (positive attitude toward literacy and preference for higher-order cognitive tasks). Liberal arts colleges in the aggregate demonstrated a positive net impact on openness to diversity and challenge, learning for self-understanding, and writing skills, while selective liberal arts colleges positively influenced not only those outcomes but also growth in reading comprehension and critical thinking. Interestingly, the impact of selective liberal arts colleges on measures of intellectual and personal growth was not shaped in a major way by the academic selectivity of their students. The presence or absence of controls for a measure of the average academic ability of an institution's students altered the estimated effects of selective liberal arts colleges in only inconsistent and minor ways.

Whether or not students attending liberal arts colleges demonstrated significant advantages over their counterparts at research universities depended on the outcome considered. On outcomes generally aimed at measuring intellectual and cognitive skills (for example, the CAAP reading comprehension, critical thinking, and writing skills tests), liberal arts college students had significant advantages over their peers at regional schools but an essential parity with students at research universities. (Even on cognitive skills such as mathematics and science reasoning, where liberal arts college students were generally disadvantaged, the deficit was smaller and less consistent in comparison with regional institutions than it was in comparison with research universities.) Conversely, on dimensions measuring students' psychosocial and attitudinal development (for example, openness to diversity, learning for self-understanding, and positive attitude toward literacy), the largest and most consistent net advantages of liberal arts colleges were found in comparison with research universities.

Although isolated exceptions existed, the clear majority of both the positive and negative total effects of liberal arts colleges on measures of intellectual and personal development were explained by differences between liberal arts colleges and other institutions in the academic and nonacademic experiences of college. This finding held not only for the positive influence of liberal arts colleges on such outcomes as openness to diversity, learning for self-understanding, writing skills, and reading comprehension but also for the negative effects of liberal arts colleges on science reasoning.

On dimensions of development such as openness to diversity, learning for self-understanding, and critical thinking, the nature of the impact of liberal arts colleges was to accentuate initial differences. Students enrolling in liberal arts colleges started postsecondary education with initially higher average scores on these variables than students at other institutions; the result of attending a liberal arts college or a selective liberal arts college was to accentuate these initial advantages even further.

Finally, although isolated exceptions existed, it was clear that most of the positive impact of liberal arts colleges on dimensions of students' intellectual and personal development occurred during the first year of postsecondary education. On some measures, such as openness to diversity and learning for self-understanding, the positive impact of liberal arts colleges continued to increase in magnitude after the first year. But even on these dimensions, the incremental impact of the first year of attendance at a liberal arts college was from 69 percent to 79 percent of the estimated impact after three years of college.

It is not readily apparent from our analyses why the consistent positive effects of liberal arts colleges on good practices in undergraduate education are not matched by equally consistent positive impacts on measures of intellectual and personal growth during college. A similar phenomenon has been observed, however, in other evidence concerning between-institution effects on the developmental outcomes of postsecondary education. Institutions with a markedly different configuration of human, financial, and educational resources do not produce similarly pronounced net differences in intellectual and personal outcomes for students (Bowen, 1977; Pascarella and Terenzini, 1991, 2005).

Several reasons may exist for this outcome. First, although the good practice variables we assessed in this investigation are uniquely linked to dimensions of students' intellectual and personal growth in the extensive literature on college impact, no necessary "if-then" relationship exists between exposure to good practices at the institutional level and development during college. Good practice dimensions clearly provide an institutional environment conducive to students' intellectual and personal growth. Differences in the extent to which institutions foster good practices, however, may not automatically lead to similar differences in developmental outcomes for all students. Indeed, recent evidence suggests that the positive impacts of good practices in undergraduate education on intellectual and personal growth differ substantially in magnitude for different kinds of students (Bray, Pascarella, and Pierson, 2004; Cruce, Pascarella, Wolniak, and Seifert, 2004).

A second possibility is that we are estimating the effects of liberal arts colleges on measures of intellectual and personal development that do not fully capture the unique impacts of liberal arts education. For example, the five tests of the CAAP assessed in the study are designed to tap the general academic skills acquired in an undergraduate education. They may not be particularly sensitive to the more complex modes of intellectual inquiry or habits of mind typically thought to be the outcomes of a liberal arts education.

Finally, institutional type (that is, liberal arts colleges, research universities, regional institutions) may simply be a structural characteristic that is too general and distal to adequately capture the full impact of liberal arts education on students' intellectual and personal growth during college. (Substantial differences in impacts among schools within each institutional type can have a dampening influence when the effects of institutional type are themselves compared.) What may count more in the explanation of students' intellectual and personal growth are environmental characteristics and individual experiences that provide a more proximal and construct-valid expression of a liberal arts experience than simply attending a liberal arts college. To test the validity of this "hypothesis," we used the theoretical and empirical literature to construct several psychometrically reliable multidimensional measures that operationalized salient components of a liberal arts education or experience. They were two aggregate measures of an institution's "liberal arts emphasis" and an individual-level measure of students' "liberal arts experiences." Net of student background characteristics, all three measures were strongly predicted by attendance at a liberal arts college—evidence of their construct validity. We found that these measures of an institution's liberal arts emphasis and students' liberal arts experiences were generally more consistent net predictors of students' intellectual and personal growth in college than was institutional type (that is, attendance at a liberal arts college versus a research university or regional institution).

Net of students' precollege characteristics, an institution's average liberal arts education emphasis had significant positive impacts (and no significant negative impacts) on a broad range of measures of intellectual and personal development during college. When additional controls for institutional selectivity and institutional type were introduced, the significant effects on measures primarily aimed at tapping cognitive growth (that is, reading comprehension, critical thinking, writing skills, and science reasoning) not only tended to persist but also increased in magnitude. Thus, the positive effects of an institution's liberal arts education emphasis on intellectual growth were not totally dependent on one's attendance at a liberal arts college. Put another way, although a liberal arts education emphasis is most likely at liberal arts colleges, it is not exclusive to those institutions. Where it is implemented and nurtured at research universities and regional institutions, it has important impacts on students' intellectual growth.

Similarly, in the presence of statistical controls for students' precollege characteristics, a student's individual-level liberal arts experience score had significant positive effects (and no negative effects) on nearly all the measures of intellectual and personal growth assessed in the study. These significant positive effects persisted even when additional statistical controls were introduced for institutional selectivity and institutional type. Thus, consistent with an institution's average liberal arts emphasis, a student's individual liberal arts experiences enhanced intellectual and personal growth irrespective of whether or not one attended a liberal arts college. The major difference was that the positive impact of an institution's average liberal arts emphasis that was independent of institutional type was largely confined to cognitively oriented outcomes. In contrast, the positive impact of a student's liberal arts experience score that was independent of institutional type existed across the full range of intellectual and personal outcomes considered.

We uncovered little evidence indicating that the positive influence of an institution's liberal arts emphasis increased discernibly in scope or magnitude after the first year of college. The positive impact of a student's liberal arts experiences appeared, however, to be more cumulative in nature, exhibiting a marked increase in magnitude from the first to the third year of college. Still, it was the case that the largest incremental impact of a student's liberal arts experiences occurred in the initial year of exposure to postsecondary education. The median effect size in the first year of college was about two-thirds of the median impact in the third year of college.

Long-Term Effects

Our analyses of the long-term effects of liberal arts colleges followed samples of alumni from private baccalaureate-level liberal arts colleges, public regional universities, and private master's level institutions located in Appalachia for five, fifteen, and twenty-five years after gradation from college. Statistically controlling for an extensive set of confounding influences, graduation from a baccalaureate liberal arts college had a number of modest but statistically significant positive total or direct impacts on long-term outcomes. Compared with demographically similar graduates of public regional universities, liberal arts college alumni not only were more satisfied with their undergraduate education but also reported that their undergraduate experience had a significantly stronger impact on their learning and intellectual development, development of leadership and self-efficacy skills, personal and spiritual development, and development of responsible citizenship. Similarly, compared with public regional university alumni, baccalaureate liberal arts college graduates had higher levels of graduate degree attainment; were more likely to be employed in a nonprofit organization and to report that their undergraduate experience prepared them for their first and current jobs; reported a higher level of religious involvement and donated a larger percentage of income to charity; took more continuing education courses for personal development and had a lower level of alcohol consumption; were more likely to be working in the

Appalachian region; and were more likely to report that learning and intellectual development, personal and spiritual growth, and responsible citizenship were important in their current lives.

Though the differences were less extensive, graduates of baccalaureate liberal arts colleges also demonstrated a number of modest but statistically significant long-term net advantages over alumni of private master's level institutions: annual salary, annual household income, religious involvement, a lower frequency of cigarette smoking, a greater likelihood of currently working in the Appalachian region and a greater number of years living and working in the Appalachian region, and a greater importance attached to learning and intellectual development in one's current life.

Most of the statistically significant net effects we uncovered favored graduates of baccalaureate liberal arts colleges over alumni of other types of institutions. A small number of negative effects were apparent, however. Compared with alumni of public regional universities, liberal arts college graduates were less likely to be employed full time, had lower annual salaries, were less likely to vote in national elections, and were less likely to campaign for a political candidate.

To some extent, we uncovered more consistent evidence of long-term effects of liberal arts colleges on the intellectual and personal development of alumni than was indicated in our analyses of the impact of liberal arts colleges on intellectual and personal growth during the college years. This finding may have both substantial and methodological explanations. From a substantive standpoint, it may be that a major part of the impact of liberal arts colleges on students' intellectual and personal development is latent and manifests itself later in an individual's personal and professional life. Thus, many aspects of intellectual and personal growth fostered by liberal arts education may be apparent to an individual only as they become relevant in his or her postcollege work and life experiences. Simply assessing change during college, as we did with the NSSL data, may overlook such latent but nonetheless significant impacts of liberal arts colleges.

At the same time, it is important to acknowledge potential methodological explanations for the results. In analyses of the NSSL data, we were able to introduce statistical controls for parallel (or close proxy) precollege measures of each outcome we considered. Though we controlled for an extensive set of demographic and other background experiences, it was not the case with the ACA data. In estimating the effects of baccalaureate liberal arts colleges (versus regional public institutions), we were not able to statistically control for an individual's precollege response propensities on instruments that asked one to indicate how much he or she was influenced by educational experiences. Consequently, our findings could also reflect the possibility that, compared with public institutions, baccalaureate liberal arts colleges simply recruited and enrolled individuals who were more open to the impacts of postsecondary education to begin with (Pascarella, 2001). The same possibility exists for the significant net impacts of baccalaureate liberal arts colleges on the importance of such factors as learning and intellectual development, personal and spiritual growth, and responsible citizenship in one's postcollegiate life. Although such effects could well reflect the distinctive long-term impacts of undergraduate education at a liberal arts college, they might also reflect the possibility that the liberal arts colleges in our sample tended to enroll students for whom these aspects of life were particularly important when they entered college.

The long-term impacts of baccalaureate liberal arts colleges on other outcomes are less ambiguous. For example, compared with alumni of public regional universities, graduates of liberal arts colleges had a higher probability of having obtained a graduate degree; this effect persisted even when precollege plans for a graduate degree were taken into account. Similarly, the positive influence of baccalaureate liberal arts colleges on graduates' probability of working in the Appalachian region persisted even after taking into account whether or not one lived in the Appalachian region when he or she graduated from high school. Because the Appalachian region is one of the most economically disadvantaged in the country, keeping a well-educated work force in the region has potentially important implications for economic development. Our findings suggest the possibility that baccalaureate liberal arts colleges may play a positive role in retaining college graduates in the Appalachian region.

There may also be less ambiguity concerning the finding that, compared with graduates of public regional universities, liberal arts college alumni were significantly more likely to report that their undergraduate experience had prepared them for both their first and their current jobs. Such a finding is not inconsistent with research conducted in the 1980s suggesting that liberal arts graduates possessed intellectual and interpersonal skills that gave them discernible advantages in adapting to job demands (see, for example, Beck, 1981; Howard, 1986; Useem, 1989).

Conditional Effects

We found little to indicate that the effects of liberal arts colleges on good practices in undergraduate education differed in magnitude for men or women, for white students or students of color, for students of different ages, or for students with different levels of precollege tested academic ability and high school extracurricular involvement. This finding suggests that the positive effects of liberal arts colleges were such that they tended to distribute exposure to, or engagement in, good practices equally to all students. Similarly, we found that the net positive or negative effects of attending a liberal arts college or a selective liberal arts college on intellectual and personal development tended to be general rather than conditional. That is, the estimated effects tended to be of equal magnitude for men and women, for white students and students of color, for students of different ages and with different levels of precollege tested academic ability, and for students who enter college with different precollege scores on each measure of intellectual and personal development considered.

In contrast with the estimated impact of attending a liberal arts college, evidence consistently indicated that the effects on intellectual and personal growth of both an institution's liberal arts emphasis and students' liberal arts experiences were conditional rather than general. Specifically, the effects varied in magnitude based on differences in precollege scores on the measures of intellectual and personal development considered in the study, race, and sex. Although not totally consistent, the clear weight of evidence indicated that an institution's liberal arts emphasis and students' liberal arts experiences may function in a compensatory manner. That is, an institution's liberal arts emphasis and students' liberal arts experiences tended to have stronger positive effects on intellectual and personal growth for students who began college relatively low on these dimensions than for their counterparts who started postsecondary education with relatively high levels of intellectual and personal development. Though less extensive, other evidence suggested that the cognitive benefits of an institution's liberal arts emphasis and students' liberal arts experiences accrued more to students of color than to their white peers and to women more than to men.

While the effects of attending a liberal arts college on good practices in undergraduate education and measures of intellectual and personal growth during college tended to be general rather than conditional, the same could not be said for the long-term impacts of graduating from a liberal arts college. Our analyses suggested that these estimated impacts differed in magnitude by sex, precollege ACT scores, and graduation cohort. Where conditional effects involved sex, it was the case that the net benefits of graduating from a baccalaureate liberal arts college (versus another type of institution) accrued more to male than to female graduates. This finding characterized the estimated effects of liberal arts colleges on such outcomes as graduate degree attainment and goals, overall satisfaction with college, percent of income donated to charity, and number of continuing education courses taken for personal development.

The conditional effects involving precollege ACT scores were consistent in suggesting that the estimated long-term effects of baccalaureate liberal arts colleges were, on certain outcomes, more pronounced for students who entered college with relatively low levels of tested academic preparation than for their counterparts with relatively high ACT scores. These outcomes included annual salary, currently living or currently working in the Appalachian region, and number of years living and working in the Appalachian region.

Finally, it is worth noting that on the vast majority of outcomes considered, the effects of graduating from a baccalaureate liberal arts college were essentially the same, irrespective of one's graduation cohort (1974–1976, 1984–1986, and 1994–1996). On several outcomes, however, the effects of liberal arts colleges differed in magnitude for older alumni (1974–1976 graduates) than for their younger counterparts (1994–1996 graduates). For example, graduating from a liberal arts college (versus another type of institution) had a stronger positive influence on one's graduate degree goal for children, the impact of the undergraduate experience on personal and spiritual development, the probability of currently being in Appalachia, and the years one lived and worked in Appalachia for older graduates (1974–1976) than for their younger counterparts (1994–1996). Conversely, the positive impact of liberal arts colleges on the development of responsible citizenship and leadership and self-efficacy skills was more pronounced for younger alumni (1994–1996) than for their older counterparts.

Conclusion

THE OPENING CHAPTER of this monograph describes the many challenges that liberal arts colleges face in the changing world of higher education. Given the increasing political and societal focus on accountability, one way for liberal arts colleges to meet these challenges is to find compelling evidence for their educational superiority. Unfortunately for these institutions, our findings are a mixed bag.

Students who attend liberal arts colleges are more likely to encounter good teaching and supportive institutional practices. Moreover, students who experience this combination of good teaching and institutional conditions, a combination that most liberal arts colleges highlight in their admissions material, show larger "value-added" gains on a variety of outcomes.

Yet it is an axiom in higher education that a distinction exists between espoused values and actual practices. This distinction is important when it comes to the relative merits of liberal arts colleges compared with other kinds of institutions. Although the teaching experiences and conditions that most liberal arts colleges value and espouse are effective, the proportion of students who *actually* experience these effective practices and conditions at these institutions was not sufficient for them to consistently produce better student outcomes. Many liberal arts college advocates also point to long-term, post-college effects as the true barometer of the impact of these institutions. Yet the modest positive effects that we identified probably would not meet hopes and expectations of advocates who believe that education at a liberal arts college creates "persons whose greatness consists in many understated virtues, persons who listen, persons who need not be ostentatious or self-aggrandizing, who need not wear their talents on their sleeves, persons who know the inner wisdom of those lines of Wordsworth about a good person's 'little, nameless, unremembered acts of kindness and love that have no slight or trivial influence on the best portion of one's life'" (Seery, 2002, p. 151).

The variability in the presence of effective teaching practices and supportive conditions across liberal arts colleges, research universities, and regional universities is similar to the variability found within institutional types in the National Survey of Student Engagement (National Survey of Student Engagement, 2004). Such variability highlights the disconnect between the convenient institutional typologies that we use in higher education and the institutional qualities that are actually relevant for students' learning. The same can be said for institutional selectivity, which does not clearly predict whether institutions enact conditions and practices that support students' learning but remains a key "quality index" for so many faculty, students, and parents (Kuh and Pascarella, 2004).

For most institutions, data indicating modest positive long-term benefits for students and the greater likelihood of supportive conditions for learning would be heartening news. Unfortunately, the impact of our findings for these institutions is tempered by the fact that liberal arts colleges often both charge *and* spend substantially more on their students than other kinds of institutions. Degree-granting public universities annually spend approximately $25,000 per student (National Center for Education Statistics, 2003). Prestigious, highly ranked liberal arts colleges annually spend more than $40,000 per student, with the very top-ranked liberal arts colleges annually spending more than $50,000 per student (Kaufman and Woglom, 2005).

Yet the focus on the financial resources of the wealthiest of these institutions blinds us to the valuable resources that are available to most liberal arts colleges regardless of the quality of their endowment, the degree of their selectivity, and the wealth of their student body. By virtue of their small size, residential environments, and public commitment to excellence in teaching, liberal arts colleges are rich in their potential for creating powerful conditions that foster students' learning. Indeed, as Kuh and others (2005) found, institutions with a wide range of financial resources can successfully engage students, provided they spend those resources wisely.

Indeed, we suggest that the factors that foster students' learning such as high-quality nonclassroom interactions with faculty, good instructional skill and clarity, and an environment that fosters academic challenge and effort for students are matters of institutional intention and commitment rather than a simple function of financial resources. That these practices are especially effective for women, students of color, and at-risk students shows the continued promise of liberal arts colleges for future generations of college students. The essential question is whether liberal arts colleges as a whole can more deeply and pervasively embrace these effective practices and conditions for their students.

According to David Labaree (2004), "A troubling fact about teaching is that there is no established set of practices that have been proven to work independent of the particular actors involved and the particular time and place of action" (p. 53). Our findings both confirm and challenge this statement. The fundamental gift of liberal arts colleges to the rest of higher education is the effectiveness of the kind of education they have long promoted. These teaching practices and institutional conditions are effective for students regardless of the type of institution where they occur. Because there are no copyrights protecting these practices, any institution is free to adopt them. Yet the significant conditional effects we uncovered in our investigation have implications for the conduct of future inquiry on the impact of liberal arts education and, more generally, for the broad field focusing on the impact of college. Research proceeding from the assumption that a common experience has the same global impact for all students risks masking important complexity in the pattern of impacts. It should come as no surprise that individual differences in the characteristics students bring to college may play a significant role in shaping the impact of the collegiate experience. Increasing diversity in the background characteristics of the American undergraduate student population makes the consideration of conditional effects in studies of college impact all the more important.

Notes

1. There is much debate over the terminology *liberal education* and *liberal arts education*. Cognizant of the history behind the terms and the meaningful albeit contentious conversations relative to the distinctions between the two, the term *liberal arts education* is here defined as "those arts, talents, skills we develop that help us to listen, speak, understand, analyze, persuade" (Agresto in Blaich, 2002) as well as to recognize and appreciate different perspectives. For the purposes of this monograph, the term *liberal arts education* is used.

2. We use the word *vocational* because of its frequent use in the literature. In our use of *vocational*, however, we refer to college or university curricula focused on professional preparation and distinguished from lower-level vocational training programs (Grubb and Lazerson, 2005).

3. By attributes of a liberal arts education, we refer to those attributes defined by Cejda and Duemer (2001), which include producing a liberally educated person, providing both breadth and a common educational experience, and developing the whole person.

4. Learning productivity was defined as "the combination of student engagement in educationally purposeful activities (such as active learning, peer cooperation, and reading and writing) and the gains they make in a range of desired outcomes (broad general education, knowledge of history, analytical and logical thinking, and science and experimentation)" (Kuh and Hu, 2001, p. 2).

5. Pace (1997) defined general liberal arts colleges as those in which 40 percent or more of degrees awarded were in traditional liberal arts disciplines but were not highly selective. Vocational liberal arts colleges were defined as those in which fewer than 40 percent of degrees awarded were in traditional liberal arts disciplines and were also not highly selective.

6. Baccalaureate Colleges–Liberal Arts and Doctoral-Extensive universities as defined by Carnegie Foundation for the Advancement of Teaching (2000).

Appendix A: Operational Definitions of Variables

Part A: Good Practices and College Experiences (NSSL Data)

Quality of nonclassroom interactions with faculty: An individual's responses on a five-item scale that assessed the quality and impact of one's nonclassroom interactions with faculty. Examples of constituent items were "Since coming to this institution, I have developed a close personal relationship with at least one faculty member," "My nonclassroom interactions with faculty have had a positive influence on my personal growth, values, and attitudes," and "My nonclassroom interactions with faculty have had a positive influence on my intellectual growth and interest in ideas." Response options were 5 = strongly agree, 4 = agree, 3 = not sure, 2 = disagree, and 1 = strongly disagree. Alpha (internal consistency) reliability = .83. The scale was summed through the first, second, or third year.

Faculty interest in teaching and student development: An individual's responses on a five-item scale that assessed students' perceptions of faculty interest in teaching and students. Examples of constituent items were "Few of the faculty members I have had contact with are genuinely interested in students" (coded in reverse), "Most of the faculty members I have had contact with are genuinely interested in teaching," and "Most of the faculty members I have had contact with are interested in helping students grow in more than just academic areas." Response options were 5 = strongly agree, 4 = agree, 3 = not sure, 2 = disagree, 1 = strongly disagree. Alpha reliability = .71. The scale was summed through the first, second, or third year.

Instructional emphasis on cooperative learning: An individual's responses on a four-item scale that assessed the extent to which the overall instruction received emphasized cooperative learning. Examples of constituent items were "I am required to work cooperatively with other students on course assignments," "In my classes, students teach each other in groups instead of only having instructors teach," and "Instructors encourage learning in student groups." Response options were 4 = very often, 3 = often, 2 = occasionally, and 1 = never. Alpha reliability = .81. The scale was summed through the first, second, or third year.

Course-related interaction with peers: An individual's responses on a ten-item scale that assessed the nature of one's interactions with peers, focusing on academic coursework. Examples of constituent items were "Studying with students from my classes," "Tried to explain the material to another student or friend," and "Attempted to explain an experimental procedure to a classmate." Response options were: 4 = very often, 3 = often, 2 = occasionally, and 1 = never. Alpha reliability = .79. The scale was summed through the first, second, or third year.

Academic effort/involvement: An individual's response on a thirty-seven-item factorially derived but modified scale that assessed one's academic effort or involvement in library experiences, experiences with faculty, course learning, and experiences in writing. The scale combined four ten-item involvement dimensions from the College Student Experiences Questionnaire (CSEQ), minus three items that were incorporated into the *course-related interaction with peers* scale described above. Examples of constituent items were "Ran down leads, looked for further references that were cited in things you read," "Did additional readings on topics that were discussed in class," and "Revised a paper or composition two or more times before you were satisfied with it." Response options were 4 = very often, 3 = often, 2 = occasionally, and 1 = never. Alpha reliability = .92. The scale was summed through the first, second, or third year.

Number of essay exams in courses: An individual's response to a single item taken from the CSEQ. Summed through the first, second, or third year.

Instructors' use of higher-order questioning techniques: An individual's responses on a four-item scale that assessed the extent to which instructors asked questions in class that required higher-order cognitive processing. Examples of constituent items were "Instructors' questions in class ask me to show how a particular course concept could be applied to an actual problem or situation," "Instructors' questions in class ask me to point out any fallacies in basic ideas, principles, or points of view presented in the course," and "Instructors' questions in class ask me to argue for or against a particular point of view." Response options were 4 = very often, 3 = often, 2 = occasionally, and 1 = never. Alpha reliability = .80. The scale was summed through the first, second, or third year.

Emphasis on higher-order examination questions: An individual's responses on a five-item scale that assessed the extent to which examination questions required higher-order cognitive processing. Examples of constituent items were "Exams require me to point out the strengths and weaknesses of a particular argument or point of view," "Exams require me to use course content to address a problem not presented in the course," and "Exams require me to compare or contrast dimensions of course content." Response options were 4 = very often, 3 = often, 2 = occasionally, and 1 = never. Alpha reliability = .77. The scale was summed through the first, second, or third year.

Using computers: An individual's response on a three-item scale indicating extent of computer use: "Using computers for class assignments," "Using computers for library searches," and "Using computers for word processing." Response options were 4 = very often, 3 = often, 2 = occasionally, and 1 = never. Alpha reliability = .65. The scale was summed through the first, second, or third year.

Instructors' feedback to students: An individual's response on a two-item scale that assessed the extent to which the overall instruction received provided feedback on student progress. The items were "Instructors keep me informed of my level of performance" and "Instructors check to see if I have learned well before going on to new material." Response options were 4 = very often, 3 = often, 2 = occasionally, and 1 = never. Alpha reliability = .70. The scale was summed through the first, second, or third year.

Course challenge/effort: An individual's responses on a six-item scale that assessed the extent to which courses and instruction received were characterized as challenging and requiring high level of effort. Examples of constituent items were "Courses are challenging and require my best intellectual effort," "Courses require more than I can get done," and "Courses require a lot of papers or laboratory reports." Response options were 4 = very often, 3 = often, 2 = occasionally, and 1 = never. Alpha reliability = .64. The scale was summed through the first, second, or third year.

Scholarly/intellectual emphasis: An individual's responses on a three-item scale that assessed perceptions of the extent to which the climate of one's college emphasized the development of academic, scholarly, and intellectual qualities; the development of esthetic, expressive, and creative qualities; or being critical, evaluative, and analytical. Response options were on a semantic differential-type scale where 7 = strong emphasis and 1 = weak emphasis. Alpha reliability = .79. The scale was summed through the first, second, or third year.

Number of textbooks or assigned readings: An individual's response to a single item taken from the CSEQ. The item was summed through the first, second, or third year.

Number of term papers or other written reports: An individual's response to a single item taken from the CSEQ. The item was summed through the first, second, or third year.

Instructional skill/clarity: An individual's responses on a five-item scale that assessed the extent to which the overall instruction received was characterized by pedagogical skill and clarity. Examples of constituent items were "Instructors give clear explanations," "Instructors make good use of examples to get across difficult points," and "Instructors interpret abstract ideas and theories clearly." Response options were 4 = very often, 3 = often, 2 = occasionally, and 1 = never. Alpha reliability = .86. The scale was summed through the first, second, or third year.

Instructional organization and preparation: An individual's responses on a five-item scale that assessed the extent to which the overall instruction received was characterized by good organization and preparation. Examples of constituent items were "Presentation of material is well organized," "Instructors are well prepared for class," and "Class time is used effectively." Response options were 4 = very often, 3 = often, 2 = occasionally, and 1 = never. Alpha reliability = .87. The scale was summed through the first, second, or third year.

Quality of interactions with students: An individual's responses on a seven-item scale that assessed the quality and impact of one's interactions with other students. Examples of constituent items were "Since coming to this institution, I have developed close personal relationships with other students," "My interpersonal relationships with other students have had positive influence on my personal growth, attitudes, and values," and "My interpersonal relationships with other students have had a positive influence on my intellectual growth and interest in ideas." Response options were 5 = strongly agree, 4 = agree, 3 = not sure, 2 = disagree, and 1 = strongly disagree. Alpha reliability = .82. The scale was summed through the first, second, or third year.

Non-course-related interactions with peers: An individual's response on a ten-item scale that assessed the nature of one's interactions with peers focusing on nonclass or nonacademic issues. Examples of constituent items were "Talked about art (painting, sculpture, architecture, artists, for example) with other students at the college," "Had serious discussions with students whose philosophy of life or personal values were very different from your own," and "Had serious discussions with students whose political opinions were very different from your own." Response items were 4 = very often, 3 = often, 2 = occasionally, and 1 = never. Alpha reliability = .84. The scale was summed through the first, second, or third year.

Cultural and interpersonal involvement: An individual's response on a thirty-eight-item factorially derived but modified scale that assessed one's effort or involvement in art, music, and theater, personal experiences, student acquaintances, and conversations with other students. The scale combined items from five involvement dimensions of the CSEQ, minus eight items that were incorporated into the *Non-Course-Related Interactions With Peers* scale described above. Examples of constituent items were "Seen a play, ballet, or other theater performance at the college," "Been in a group where each person, including yourself, talked about his/her personal problems," "Made friends with students whose interests were different from yours," "Had conversations with other students about major social problems such as peace, human rights, equality, and justice," and "In conversations with other students, explored different ways of thinking about the topic." Response options were 4 = very often, 3 = often,

2 = occasionally, and 1 = never. Alpha reliability = .92. The scale was summed through the first, second, or third year.

Emphasis on supportive interactions with others: An individual's responses on a three-item scale that assessed the extent to which one's relationships with faculty, administrators/staff, and other students could be described as friendly, supportive, helpful, or flexible (coded 7) to competitive, remote, impersonal, or rigid (coded 1). Alpha reliability = .70. The scale was summed through the first, second, or third year.

Extracurricular involvement: An individual's response on a thirty-item factorially derived scale that assessed one's effort or involvement in campus union activities, campus clubs, and campus athletic and recreational facilities. The scale combined three ten-item involvement dimensions from the CSEQ. Examples of constituent items were "Heard a speaker at the student union or center," "Worked in some student organization or special project (publications, student government, social event, for example)," and "Played on an intramural team." Response options were 4 = very often, 3 = often, 2 = occasionally, and 1 = never. Alpha reliability = .92. The scale was summed through the first, second, or third year.

Integration of ideas: An individual's response on a three-item scale that assessed one's effort or involvement in integrating ideas. The constituent items were "Tried to see how different facts and ideas fit together," "Worked on a paper or project where you had to integrate ideas from various sources," and "Gained in ability to put ideas together, to see relationships, similarities, and differences between ideas." Response options were 4 = very often, 3 = often, 2 = occasionally, and 1 = never for the first two items, and 4 = very much, 3 = quite a bit, 2 = some, and 1 = very little for the third item. Alpha reliability = .62.

Cumulative credit hours completed: Cumulative number of credit hours completed through the first, second, or third year.

Average hours per week spent studying: Single-item, six-point self-report of average hours spent studying per week, where 1 = none and 6 = more than 20 hours (summed through the first, second, or third year).

Social sciences courses taken: Cumulative number of college courses taken through the first, second, or third year in anthropology, audiology/speech pathology, child and family services, communications, economics, geography, history, political science, psychology, sociology, or social work.

Mathematics courses taken: Cumulative number of college courses taken through the first, second, or third year in prealgebra, algebra, calculus, statistics, computer science, geometry, matrix algebra, accounting, or business math.

Technical/preprofessional courses taken: Cumulative number of college courses taken through the first, second, or third year in drawing, drafting, architectural design, criminology, education, agriculture, business, physical therapy, pharmacy, physical education, nursing, or computer programming.

Arts and humanities courses taken: Cumulative number of college courses taken through the first, second, or third year in art history, art appreciation, studio art, dance, theater, music appreciation, music performance, composition of writing, English literature, foreign language, humanities, philosophy, linguistics, classics, or religious studies.

Natural sciences courses taken: Cumulative number of college courses taken through the first, second, or third year in astronomy, botany, chemistry, physics, geology, zoology, and microbiology.

Hours worked per week on campus: Average number of hours of on-campus work per week during the school year, where 1 = none to 9 = more than 35. The item was summed through the first, second, or third year.

Hours worked per week off campus: Average number of hours of off-campus work per week during the school year, where 1 = none to 9 = more than 35. The item was summed through the first, second, or third year.

On-campus residence: A dummy variable where 1 = lived on campus and 0 = lived off campus and commuted. The item was summed through the first, second, or third year.

Intercollegiate athletics: A dummy variable where 1 = participated in an intercollegiate sport and 0 = did not participate in an intercollegiate sport. The item was summed through the first, second, or third year.

Greek affiliation: A dummy variable where 1 = joined a fraternity or sorority and 0 = remained independent. The item was summed through the first, second, or third year.

Volunteer work: A single item that asked the students how often during the school year they had engaged in volunteer work. Response options were

4 = very often, 3 = often, 2 = occasionally, and 1 = never. The item was summed through the first, second, or third year.

Part B: Outcome Measures (NSSL Data)

Reading comprehension: An individual's score on the Collegiate Assessment of Academic Proficiency (CAAP) reading comprehension module, a forty-minute multiple-choice test comprising thirty-six items that assesses reading comprehension as a product of skill in inferring, reasoning, and generalizing. The test consists of four 900-word prose passages designed to represent the level and kinds of reading students commonly encounter in college curricula, including topics in fiction, humanities, social sciences, and natural sciences. Alpha reliabilities range from .76 to .87.

Mathematics knowledge: An individual's score on the CAAP mathematics module, a forty-minute multiple-choice test comprising thirty-five items designed to measure a student's ability to solve mathematical problems. The test emphasizes quantitative reasoning rather than formal memorization and includes algebra (four levels), coordinate geometry, trigonometry, and introductory calculus. Alpha reliabilities range from .79 to .81.

Critical thinking skills: An individual's score on the CAAP critical thinking module, a forty-minute multiple-choice test comprising thirty-two items. It is designed to measure a student's ability to clarify, analyze, evaluate, and extend arguments. The test consists of four passages in a variety of formats (for example, case studies, debates, dialogues, experimental results, statistical arguments, and editorials). Each passage contains a series of arguments that support a general conclusion. Alpha reliabilities range from .81 to .82.

Science reasoning: An individual's score on the CAAP science reasoning module, a forty-minute multiple-choice test comprising forty-five items. The contents of the test are drawn from biology, chemistry, physics, and the physical sciences (geology, astronomy, and meteorology). The test emphasizes scientific reasoning skills rather than recall of scientific content or a high level of skill in mathematics or reading. It consists of eight passages, each of which contains scientific information and a set of multiple-choice test questions. Response stimuli for the passages include data representation (graphic and tabular material similar to those found in science journals and texts), research summaries (descriptions of one or several experiments), and conflicting viewpoints (students are presented with several hypotheses or views that are mutually inconsistent because of different premises, incomplete or disputed data, or different interpretations of data). Alpha reliabilities range from .76 to .87.

Writing skills: An individual's score on the CAAP writing skills module, a forty-minute multiple-choice test comprising seventy-two items. The test measures a student's understanding of the conventions of standard written English in use and mechanics (punctuation, grammar, and sentence structure) and rhetorical skills (strategy, organization, and style). Spelling, vocabulary, and rote recall of grammatical rules are not tested. The test consists of six prose passages, each of which is accompanied by a set of twelve multiple-choice test items. A range of passage types is used to provide a variety of rhetorical situations. Items that measure use and mechanics offer alternative responses, including *no change,* to underlined portions of the test. The student must decide which alternative employs the conventional practice in use and mechanics that best fits the context. Items that measure rhetorical skills may refer to an underlined portion of the test or may ask a question about a section of the passage or about the passage as a whole. The student must decide which alternative response is most appropriate in a given rhetorical situation. Alpha reliabilities range from .93 to .95.

Plans to obtain a graduate degree: An individual's response to the question "What is the highest academic degree you intend to obtain in your lifetime?" Coded 1 = master's degree or above, 0 = bachelor's degree or below.

Openness to diversity and challenge: An individual's score on an eight-item Likert-type scale (5 = strongly agree to 1 = strongly disagree) that assesses openness to cultural, racial, and value diversity as well the extent to which one enjoys being challenged by different perspectives, values, and ideas. Constituent items were "I enjoy having discussions with people whose ideas and values are different from my own," "The real value of a college education lies in being introduced to different values," "I enjoy talking with people who have values different from mine because it helps me understand myself and my values better," "Learning about people from different cultures is a very important part of my college education," "I enjoy taking courses that challenge my beliefs and values," "The courses I enjoy the most are those that make me think about things from a different perspective," "Contact with individuals whose background (such as race, national origin, sexual orientation) is different from my own is an essential part of my college education," and "I enjoy courses that are intellectually challenging." Alpha reliabilities ranged from .83 to .84.

Learning for self-understanding: An individual's score on a three-item Likert-type scale (5 = strongly agree to 1 = strongly disagree) that assesses the importance of learning about oneself during college. Constituent items were "One of the most important benefits of a college education is a better understanding of myself and my values," "Developing a clear sense of who I am is very important to me," and "I prefer courses in which the material helps me understand something about myself." Alpha reliabilities ranged from .73 to .76.

Internal locus of attribution for academic success: An individual's score on a four-item Likert-type scale (5 = strongly agree to 1 = strongly disagree) that assesses the extent to which one feels that academic success in college is based on individual hard work or effort rather than on luck or external circumstances. Constituent items (coded in reverse) were "The grade I get in a course depends on how hard the instructor grades, not on how carefully I study," "Good luck is more important for college academic success than hard work," "Getting a good grade in a college course depends more on being 'naturally smart' than on how hard I work," and "When I have trouble learning the material in a course it is because the professor isn't doing a very good job." Alpha reliabilities ranged from .62 to .69.

Preference for higher-order cognitive tasks: An individual's score on a two-item Likert-type scale (5 = strongly agree to 1 = strongly disagree) that assessed one's preference for higher-order cognitive tasks. Constituent items were "I prefer exams requiring me to organize and interpret information or ideas over exams that ask me only to remember facts or information" and "I prefer to do assignments in which I have to analyze and interpret what I've just read rather than just summarize and report." Alpha reliabilities ranged from .65 to .68.

Positive attitude toward literacy: An individual's score on a seven-item Likert-type scale (5 = strongly agree to 1 = strongly disagree) that assessed a positive attitude toward reading and writing. Constituent items were "I enjoy reading poetry and literature," "I enjoy reading about science," "I enjoy reading about history," "I enjoy expressing my ideas in writing," "After I write about something, I see that subject differently," "I prefer readings that are relevant to my personal experience," and "If I have something to read, I'm never bored." Alpha reliabilities ranged from .70 to .73.

Part C: Outcome Measures (ACA Data)

Current graduate degree attainment: Highest educational degree earned at any college, coded 1 = master's degree or higher, 0 = bachelor's degree or lower.

   Current lifetime graduate degree goal: Highest educational degree to which one currently aspires, coded 1 = master's degree or higher, 0 = bachelor's degree or lower.

   Graduate degree goal for children: Highest educational degree goal for dependent children, coded 1 = master's degree or higher, 0 = bachelor's degree or lower.

   Undergraduate college's impact on learning and intellectual development: A seven-item scale measuring alumni perceptions of their undergraduate college's contribution to learning and cognitive development. Examples of constituent items were "Improving thinking and reasoning skills," "Developing problem-solving skills," and "Engaging in life-long learning." Items coded 5 = very great, 4 = great, 3 = moderate, 2 = little, and 1 = none. Alpha reliability = .86.

   Undergraduate college's impact on the development of leadership/self-efficacy skills: A nine-item scale measuring alumni perceptions of the contribution of their undergraduate college to the development of leadership and self-efficacy skills. Examples of constituent items were "Developing leadership skills," "Working as a team member," and "Developing time management skills." Items coded 5 = very great to 1 = none. Alpha reliability = .89.

   Undergraduate college's impact on personal and spiritual development: A five-item scale measuring alumni perceptions of the contribution of their undergraduate college to personal and spiritual development. Examples of constituent items were "Developing ethical standards," "Developing religious values," and "Actively participating in volunteer work to support worthwhile causes." Items coded 5 = very great to 1 = none. Alpha reliability = .83.

Undergraduate college's impact on the development of responsible citizenship: A four-item scale measuring alumni perceptions of the contribution of their undergraduate college to the development of responsible citizenship. Examples of constituent items were "Exercising my rights, responsibilities, and privileges as a citizen," "Understanding international issues," and "Interacting well with people from social groups or cultures different from my own." Items coded 5 = very great to 1 = none. Alpha reliability = .78.

Undergraduate college's impact on the development of scientific and quantitative skills: A three-item scale measuring alumni perceptions of the contribution of their undergraduate college to the development of scientific and quantitative skills. Constituent items were "Applying scientific knowledge and skills," "Applying mathematics and statistics," and "Applying computer skills and related technology." Items coded 5 = very great to 1 = none. Alpha reliability = .68.

Overall satisfaction with college: A single item asking alumni to indicate their overall satisfaction with their undergraduate college. Coded 5 = very satisfied to 1 = very dissatisfied.

Employed full-time: A single-item categorical variable indicating if one were currently employed full time. Coded 1 = employed full-time and 0 = not employed full time.

Employed in a for-profit organization or business: A single-item categorical variable indicating if one were currently employed in a for-profit organization or business. Coded 1 = employed in a for-profit organization or business and 0 = not employed in a for-profit organization or business.

Extent to which undergraduate experiences prepared one for his or her first or current job: Two single items measuring alumni perceptions of the extent to which their undergraduate experiences prepared them for their first job after graduating from college and their current job. Coded 6 = exceptionally well to 1 = not at all.

Annual salary: A single item asking alumni to indicate their annual salary or income for the most recent year. Coded 1 = none to 11 = $125,000 or more.

Annual total household income: A single item asking alumni to indicate their total household income for the most recent year. Coded 1 = none to 11 = $125,000 or more.

Satisfaction with job autonomy: A four-item scale measuring alumni ratings of satisfaction with the degree of autonomy they have in their current job. Examples of constituent items were "Satisfaction with autonomy and independence," "Satisfaction with opportunities to participate in decision making," and "Satisfaction with opportunities to exercise initiative." Items coded 5 = very satisfied, 4 = satisfied, 3 = neither satisfied nor dissatisfied, 2 = dissatisfied, 1 = very dissatisfied. Alpha reliability = .88.

Satisfaction with personal fulfillment from job: A three-item scale measuring alumni ratings of satisfaction with the degree of personal fulfillment they derive from their current job. Constituent items were "Satisfaction with feelings of accomplishment," "Satisfaction with intellectual challenge," and "Satisfaction with social status or recognition." Items coded 5 = very satisfied to 1 = very dissatisfied. Alpha reliability = .80.

Satisfaction with financial characteristics of job: A four-item scale measuring alumni ratings of satisfaction with the financial characteristics of their current job. Examples of constituent items were "Satisfaction with salary," "Satisfaction with fringe benefits," and "Satisfaction with opportunities for advancement." Items coded 5 = very satisfied to 1 = very dissatisfied. Alpha reliability = .73.

Community and social involvement: A six-item scale measuring the frequency of alumni involvement in their community and in social groups. Examples of constituent items were "Current participation in political or civic organizations," "Current participation in youth activities," and "Current participation in cultural/arts organizations. Items coded 1 = 0 hours per week, 2 = 1–5 hours per week, 3 = 6–10 hours per week, 4 = 11–15 hours per week, and 5 = more than 15 hours per week. Alpha reliability = .69.

Religious involvement: A single item measuring the frequency of alumni involvement in religious activities. Coded 1 = 0 hours per week to 5 = more than 15 hours per week.

Voting in local elections: A single item asking alumni to indicate the frequency they vote in local elections. Coded 5 = almost always, 4 = usually, 3 = occasionally, 2 = rarely, 1 = never.

Voting in state elections: A single item asking alumni to indicate the frequency they vote in state elections. Coded 5 = almost always to 1 = never.

Voting in national elections: A single item asking alumni to indicate the frequency they vote in national elections. Coded 5 = almost always to 1 = never.

Run for political office: A single-item categorical variable coded 1 = yes, 0 = no.

Been appointed to a political office: A single-item categorical variable coded 1 = yes, 0 = no.

Been elected to a political office: A single-item categorical variable coded 1 = yes, 0 = no.

Campaigned for or assisted someone running for political office: A single-item categorical variable coded 1 = yes, 0 = no.

Percent of income saved: A single item asking alumni to estimate the average percentage of family income saved (put into savings, investments, retirement accounts, and so forth). Coded 1 = 0%, 2 = 1–5%, 3 = 6–10%, 4 = 11–15%, 5 = 16–20%, and 6 = more than 20%.

Percent of income donated to charity: A single item asking alumni to estimate the average percentage of family income donated to charitable organizations (such as United Way, church/religious organizations, civic/political organizations). Coded 1 = 0% to 6 = more than 20%.

Number of continuing education courses taken for career or professional advancement: A single item asking alumni to indicate the number of continuing education courses they have taken for career or professional advancement. Coded 1 = 0, 2 = 1–3, 3 = 4–6, and 4 = 7 or more.

Number of continuing education courses taken for personal development: A single item asking alumni to indicate the number of continuing education courses they have taken for personal development. Coded 1 = 0 to 4 = 7 or more.

Current health status: A single item asking alumni how they would rate their health. Coded 5 = excellent, 4 = good, 3 = fair, 2 = poor, 1 = very poor.

Frequency of alcoholic beverage consumption: A single item asking alumni how frequently they consume alcoholic beverages (beer, wine, hard liquor). Coded 1 = I don't consume alcoholic beverages, 2 = less than one drink per day, 3 = 1–2 drinks per day, 4 = 3–4 drinks per day, and 5 = more than 4 drinks per day.

Frequency of cigarette smoking: A single item asking alumni how frequently they smoke cigarettes. Coded 1 = I don't smoke cigarettes, 2 = 1–10 cigarettes per day, 3 = 11–20 cigarettes per day, 4 = 21–30 cigarettes per day, and 5 = more than 30 cigarettes per day.

Frequency of aerobic exercise: A single item asking alumni to indicate how often they engage in aerobic exercise (running, walking, hiking, swimming). Coded 1 = I don't exercise regularly, 2 = 1–2 hours per week, 3 = 3–4 hours per week, 4 = 5–6 hours per week, and 5 = more than 6 hours per week.

Sense of control over life events: A single item asking alumni to rate how much control they felt they had over important events in their lives. The rating was on a five-point scale, where 1 = little or no control, 3 = moderate control, and 5 = a great deal of control.

Satisfaction with life: A five-item scale measuring alumni perceptions of satisfaction with their current lives. Examples of constituent items were "Satisfaction with overall life," "Satisfaction with family relationships," and "Satisfaction with social/friendship relationships." Items coded 5 = very satisfied to 1 = very dissatisfied. Alpha reliability = .81.

Currently live in the Appalachian region: A single item asking alumni to refer to a map provided of the Appalachian region and to indicate whether or not they were currently living in the Appalachian region. Coded 1 = yes, 0 = no.

Currently work in the Appalachian region: A single item asking alumni to refer to a map provided of the Appalachian region and to indicate whether or not they were currently working in the Appalachian region. Coded 1 = yes, 0 = no.

Number of years living in the Appalachian region: A single item asking alumni to refer to the map provided and respond to the question, Since earning your bachelor's degree, for how many years have you lived in the Appalachian region? Coded 1 = 0 years, 2 = 1–5 years, 3 = 6–10 years, 4 = 11–15 years, and 5 = 16 or more years.

Number of years working in the Appalachian region: A single item asking alumni to refer to the map provided and respond to the question, Since earning your bachelor's degree, for how many years have you worked in the

Appalachian region? Coded 1 = 0 years, 2 = 1–5 years, 3 = 6–10 years, 4 = 11–15 years, and 5 = 16 or more years.

Importance of learning and intellectual development in one's current endeavors: A seven-item scale measuring alumni perceptions of the importance of learning and intellectual development in one's current endeavors. Items were the same as in the parallel college impact scales previously described. Items coded 5 = very great to 1 = none. Alpha reliability = .82.

Importance of leadership/self-efficacy skills in one's current endeavors: A nine-item scale measuring alumni perceptions of the importance of leadership/self-efficacy skills in one's current endeavors. Items were the same as in the parallel college impact scales previously described. Items coded 5 = very great to 1 = none. Alpha reliability = .85.

Importance of personal and spiritual development in one's current endeavors: A five-item scale measuring alumni perceptions of the importance of personal and spiritual development in one's current endeavors. Items were the same as in the parallel college impact scales previously described. Items coded 5 = very great to 1 = none. Alpha reliability = .80.

Importance of responsible citizenship in one's current endeavors: A four-item scale measuring alumni perceptions of the importance of responsible citizenship in one's current endeavors. Items were the same as in the parallel college impact scales previously described. Items coded 5 = very great to 1 = none. Alpha reliability = .72.

Importance of scientific/quantitative skills in one's current endeavors: A three-item scale measuring alumni perceptions of the importance of scientific/quantitative skills in one's current endeavors. Items were the same as in the parallel college impact scales previously described. Items coded 5 = very great to 1 = none. Alpha reliability = .62.

Appendix B: Statistical Controls Introduced in the Analysis of Different Study Outcomes

Twenty-One Measures of Good Practices in Undergraduate Education (NSSL Data)

Tested precollege academic ability (composite of Collegiate Assessment of Academic Proficiency [CAAP] reading comprehension, mathematics, and critical thinking test scores); the average tested precollege academic ability (composite of CAAP reading comprehension, mathematics, and critical thinking test scores) of students entering each institution; precollege educational plans; a measure of precollege academic motivation; college attended was one's first choice; age; sex; race; parents' education and income; secondary school grades; time spent during secondary school in eight separate activities (studying, socializing with friends, talking with teachers outside class, working for pay, exercising or sports, studying with friends, volunteer work, and extracurricular activities); on-campus versus off-campus residence; and cumulative number of credit hours completed. In the second-year analyses, each equation also included a student's first-year score on each good practice variable. In the third-year analyses, each equation also included a student's cumulative first- and second-year score on each good practice measure.

Eleven Measures of Student Intellectual and Personal Development During College (NSSL Data)

Tested precollege academic ability (composite of CAAP reading comprehension, mathematics, and critical thinking) or a parallel pretest for the prediction of reading comprehension, mathematics, or critical thinking; the average tested precollege academic ability (composite of CAAP reading comprehension, mathematics, and critical thinking) of students at the institution attended; precollege plans to obtain a graduate degree; a measure of precollege academic motivation; college attended was first choice; age; sex; race; parents' education; parents' income; secondary school grades; time spent during high school working for pay; a scale consisting of time spent during high school in seven activities (studying, socializing with friends, talking with teachers outside class, exercising or sports, studying with friends, volunteer work, and extracurricular activities); and an exact parallel precollege measure of each outcome except writing skills and science reasoning. For these last two outcomes, the major control variable was tested precollege academic ability, which correlated .77 with writing skills and .72 with science reasoning.

All Long-Term Outcomes (ACA Study Data)

Basic Controls

ACT composite (English and mathematics) score; precollege graduate degree plans; secondary school grades; age; race; sex; parents' educational attainment; parents' income; college attended was first choice; precollege expectations to apply for financial aid; dummy variables representing graduation cohort (1974–76, 1984–86, 1994–96); whether or not one lived in the Appalachian region when graduating from high school; and the academic selectivity of the institution attended (that is, the average ACT composite score of students). These controls were introduced in all analyses of the ACA study data and are hereafter referred to as "basic controls."

Additional Controls

In addition to the basic controls introduced in all analyses, controls for a number of other influences were introduced in the analyses of certain outcomes, including college grades; graduate degree attainment; marital status; seven dummy variables representing college major (health sciences and related fields, business-related fields, biological and physical sciences, social sciences, arts and humanities, technical and applied fields, and science and engineering); five college impact scales (learning and intellectual development, entrepreneurial skills, personal and spiritual development, responsible citizenship, and scientific/quantitative skills); congruence between major and job; employment status; income; and health status in college. For each outcome analyzed, the specific controls introduced are indicated.

References

Adelman, C. (1998, November). *Institutional effects in an age of multi-institutional attendance.* Paper presented at the annual meeting of the Association for the Study of Higher Education, Miami, FL.

Ahson, N., Gentemann, K., and Phelps, P. (1998, May). *Do stop outs return? A longitudinal study of reenrollment, attrition, and graduation.* Paper presented at the annual forum of the Association of Institutional Research, Minneapolis, MN.

Aleman, A.M.M., and Salkever, K. (2002, April). *Multiculturalism and the liberal arts college: Faculty perceptions of pedagogy.* Paper presented at the annual meeting of the American Educational Research Association, New Orleans, LA.

Alwin, D., and Hauser, R. (1975). The decomposition of effects in path analysis. *American Sociological Review, 40*(1), 37–47.

American Association for Liberal Education. (2004). *The academy's educational standards.* Retrieved June 25, 2004, from http://www.aale.org/edstand.htm.

American Association of State Colleges and Universities. (1976). *Value-centered education and moral commitment.* Washington, DC: American Association of State Colleges and Universities.

American College Testing Program. (1990). *Report on the technical characteristics of CAAP. Pilot year 1: 1988–89.* Iowa City: American College Testing Program.

American College Testing Program. (2002). *National collegiate dropout and graduation rates.* Iowa City: Office for the Enhancement of Educational Practices, American College Testing Program.

Anaya, G. (1999, April). *Within-college, curricular and co-curricular correlates of performance on the MCAT.* Paper presented at the annual meeting of the American Educational Research Association, Montreal, QC.

Arnold, J., Kuh, G., Vesper, N., and Schuh, J. (1993). Student age and enrollment status as determinants of learning and personal development at metropolitan institutions. *Journal of College Student Development, 34*(1), 11–16.

Association of American Colleges and Universities (1998, October). *Statement on liberal learning.* Retrieved June 28, 2004, from http://www.aacu-edu.org/About/liberal_learning.cfm.

Astin, A. (1993). *What matters in college?* San Francisco: Jossey-Bass.

Astin, A. (1999). How the liberal arts college affects students. *Daedalus, 128*(1), 77–100.

Astin, A. (2000). How the liberal arts college affects students. In S. G. Koblik and S. R. Graubard (Eds.), *Distinctively American: The residential liberal arts colleges* (pp. 77–100). New Brunswick, NJ: Transaction Publishers.

Astin, A., and Lee, C. (1972). *The invisible colleges.* New York: McGraw-Hill.

Astin, A., and Lee, J. (2003). How risky are one-shot cross-sectional assessments of undergraduate students? *Research in Higher Education, 44*(6), 657–672.

Atkinson, D. (1997). The state of liberal education. *Liberal Education, 83*(2), 48–54.

Atkinson, D., Swanson, D., and Reardon, M. (1998). The state of liberal education: Part 2. Assessing institutional perspective. *Liberal Education, 84*(2), 26–31.

Barker, C. (2000). *Liberal arts education for a global society.* New York: Carnegie Corporation of New York.

Beck, R. (1981). *Career patterns: The liberal arts major in Bell System management.* Washington, DC: Association of American Colleges.

Bellas, M. (1998). *Investments in education: Do returns diminish with age?* Paper presented at the annual meeting of the American Educational Research Association, San Diego, CA.

Bird, C. (1975). *The case against college.* New York: McKay.

Blaich, C. (2002, September 29). *Provisional operational definition of the liberal arts.* Available from the Center of Inquiry in the Liberal Arts at Wabash College, P.O. Box 352, Crawfordsville, IN 47933.

Blaich, C., Bost, A., Chan, E., and Lynch, R. (2004). *Defining liberal arts education.* Retrieved September 7, 2004, from http://www.liberalarts.wabash.edu/cila/home.cfm?news_id=1401#14.

Boehner, J., and McKeon, H. (2003). *The college cost crisis: A congressional analysis of college costs and implications for America's higher education system.* (ED 479 752)

Bonvillian, G., and Murphy, R. (1996). *The liberal arts college adapting to change: The survival of small schools.* New York: Garland Publishing.

Bowen, H. (1977). *Investment in learning.* San Francisco: Jossey-Bass.

Bowen, W., and Bok, D. (1998). *The shape of the river: Long-term consequences of considering race in college and university admissions.* Princeton, NJ: Princeton University Press.

Bray, G., Pascarella, E., and Pierson, C. (2004). Postsecondary education and some dimensions of literacy development: An exploration of longitudinal evidence. *Reading Research Quarterly, 39,* 306–330.

Breneman, D. (1990). Are we losing our liberal arts colleges? *College Board Review, 150,* 16–21.

Breneman, D. (1994a). For whom is liberal education produced? *New Directions for Higher Education, 85,* 53–59.

Breneman, D. (1994b). *Liberal arts colleges: Thriving, surviving, or endangered?* Washington, DC: Brookings Institution.

Brint, S. (2002). The rise of the "practical arts." In S. Brint (Ed.), *The future of the city of intellect* (pp. 231–259). Stanford, CA: Stanford University Press.

Brown, F. (1979). Toward a better definition of liberal education: Seven perspectives. *Liberal Education, 65*(3), 383–391.

Cabrera, A., and others. (2002). Collaborative learning: Its impact on college students' development and diversity. *Journal of College Student Development, 43*(1), 20–34.

Carini, R., and Kuh, G. (2003). *2002 NSSE-RAND construct-validation study: Some insights into the role of student engagement to student learning.* Bloomington: Indiana University Center for Postsecondary Research.

Carnegie Foundation for the Advancement of Teaching. (2000). *The 2000 Carnegie classification: Background and description.* Retrieved February 26, 2004, from http://www.carnegiefoundation.org/Classification/CIHE2000/background.htm.

Carnevale, A., and Strohl, J. (2001). The demographic window of opportunity: Liberal education in the new century. *Peer Review, 3*(2), 10–13.

Cejda, B., and Duemer, L. (2001, April). *The curriculum in liberal arts colleges: Beyond the major.* Paper presented at the annual meeting of the American Educational Research Association, Seattle, WA.

Center of Inquiry in the Liberal Arts. (2004). *Understanding liberal arts education.* Retrieved July 1, 2004, from http://www.liberalarts.wabash.edu/cila/researchers.

Chickering, A. (1969). *Education and identity.* San Francisco: Jossey-Bass.

Chickering, A. (1982). Liberal education and work. *National Forum: Phi Kappa Phi Journal, 62*(2), 22–23.

Chickering, A., and Gamson, Z. (1987). Seven principles for good practice in undergraduate education. *AAHE Bulletin, 39*(7), 3–7.

Chickering, A., and Gamson, Z. (1991). *Applying the seven principles for good practice in undergraduate education.* San Francisco: Jossey-Bass.

Chickering, A., and Reisser, L. (1993). *Education and identity* (2nd ed.). San Francisco: Jossey-Bass.

Clark, B., and others. (1972). *Students and colleges: Interaction and change.* Berkeley: Center for Research and Development in Higher Education, University of California.

College Placement Council. (1975). *Four-year liberal arts graduates: Their utilization in business, industry, and government. The problem and some solutions.* Bethlehem, PA: College Placement Council.

Conrad, C., and Wyer, J. (1982). *Seven trends in liberal learning.* Washington, DC: Association of Governing Boards of Universities and Colleges.

Consortium for Student Retention Data Exchange. (2002). *CSRDE Retention Report.* Norman: Center for Institutional Data Exchange and Analysis, University of Oklahoma.

Cronon, W. (1999). "Only connect": The goals of a liberal education. *Liberal Education, 85*(1), 6–12.

Cruce, T., Pascarella, E., Wolniak, G., and Seifert, T. (2004, November). *Impacts of good practices on learning orientations, cognitive development, and graduate degree plans during the first year of college.* Paper presented at the annual meeting of the Association for the Study of Higher Education, Kansas, MO.

d'Apollonia, S., and Abrami, P. (1997). Navigating student ratings of instruction. *American Psychologist, 52*(11), 1198–1208.

Davis, T., and Murrell, P. (1993). A structural model of perceived academic, personal, and vocational gains related to college student responsibility. *Research in Higher Education, 34*, 267–289.

Delucchi, M. (1997). "Liberal arts" colleges and the myth of uniqueness. *Journal of Higher Education, 68*(4), 414–426.

Douzenis, C. (1996). The relationship of quality of effort and estimate of knowledge gain among community college students. *Community College Review, 24*(3), 27–35.

Durden, W. (2002). Liberal arts for all. *Trusteeship, 10*(2), 25–28.

Durden, W. (2003, July 18). The liberal arts as a bulwark of business education. *Chronicle of Higher Education, 49*(45), B20.

Ethington, C. (1998, November). *Influences of the normative environment of peer groups on community college students' perceptions of growth and development.* Paper presented at the annual meeting of the Association for the Study of Higher Education, Miami, FL.

Feldman, K. (1994). *Identifying exemplary teaching: Evidence from course and teacher evaluations.* Paper commissioned by the National Center on Postsecondary Teaching, Learning, and Assessment. Stony Brook, NY: SUNY at Stony Brook.

Feldman, K. (1997). Identifying exemplary teachers and teaching: Evidence from student ratings. In R. Perry and J. Smart (Eds.), *Effective teaching in higher education: Research and practice* (pp. 368–395). Edison, NJ: Agathon Press.

Finkelstein, M., Seal, R., and Schuster, J. (1998). *The new academic generation: A profession in transformation.* Baltimore: The Johns Hopkins University Press.

Fitzgerald, R. (2000). *College quality and the earnings of recent college graduates* (NCES Report No. 2000–043). Washington, DC: National Center for Education Statistics, U.S. Department of Education.

Freedman, J. (2000, Spring). On a liberal education: Have our curricula been adulterated by vocationalism? *Spectator, 33*, 10–11.

Frieden Graham, G. (1989). *Making meaning of a liberal arts experience: A longitudinal investigation of student change in intellectual and ethical development.* Unpublished doctoral dissertation, Memphis State University, Memphis, TN.

Frost, S. (1991). Fostering the critical thinking of college women through academic advising and faculty contact. *Journal of College Student Development, 32*(4), 359–366.

Good, J., and Cartwright, C. (1998). Development of moral judgment among undergraduate university students. *College Student Journal, 32*(2), 270–276.

Goodchild, L., and Wechsler, H. (Eds.). (1828/1997). The Yale report. In *Association for the Study of Higher Education reader on the history of higher education* (2nd ed., pp. 171–178). Needham Heights, MA: Ginn Press.

Goodchild, L., and Wechsler, H. (Eds.). (1947/1989). Report of the president's commission on higher education for democracy, 1947. In *Association for the Study of Higher Education reader on the history of higher education* (2nd ed., pp. 630–648). Needham Heights, MA: Ginn Press.

Gorelick, S. (1982). Critical needs: Education and work for a world in crisis. *Community Review, 4*(2), 6–13.

Graham, S. (1998). Adult growth in college: The effects of age and educational ethos. *Journal of College Student Development, 39*(3), 239–250.

Grayson, J. (1999). The impact of university experiences on self-assessed skills. *Journal of College Student Development, 40*(6), 687–699.

Green, C. S., III, and Salem, R. (1988, Spring). Assessing the prospects for liberal learning and careers. *New Directions for Teaching and Learning,* 5–19.

Grubb, W. N., and Lazerson, M. (2005). Vocationalism in higher education: The triumph of the education gospel. *Journal of Higher Education, 76*(1), 1–25.

Hagedorn, L., and others. (1999). Institutional context and the development of critical thinking: A research note. *Review of Higher Education, 22*(3), 247–263.

Hagedorn, L., Siadat, M., Nora, A., and Pascarella, E. (1997). Factors leading to gains in mathematics during the first year of college. *Journal of Women and Minorities in Science and Engineering, 3*(3), 185–202.

Hake, R. (1998). Interactive engagement versus traditional methods: A six-thousand student survey of mechanics test data for introductory physics courses. *American Journal of Physics, 66*(1), 64–74.

Hawkins, H. (2000). The making of the liberal arts college identity. In S. Koblik and S. R. Graubard (Eds.), *Distinctively American: The residential liberal arts colleges* (pp. 1–25). New Brunswick, NJ: Transaction Publishers.

Hayek, J., and Kuh, G. (1998, November). *The capacity for life-long learning of college seniors in the mid-1980s to the mid-1990s.* Paper presented at the annual meeting of the Association for the Study of Higher Education, Miami, FL.

Healy, T. (1980). A critique of uncriticized assumptions. *Liberal Education, 66*(2), 141–147.

Heath, D. (1968). *Growing up in college: Liberal education and maturity.* San Francisco: Jossey-Bass.

Heath, D. (1976). What the enduring effects of higher education tell us about a liberal education. *Journal of Higher Education, 47*(2), 173–190.

Heller, D. (Ed.). (2001). *The states and public higher education policy: Affordability, access, and accountability.* Baltimore: Johns Hopkins University Press.

Hersh, R. (1997). Intentions and perceptions. *Change, 29*(2), 16–23.

Hill, B. (1994). The nature of liberal education today. *New Directions for Higher Education, 85*(7), 7–11.

Hines, C., Cruickshank, D., and Kennedy, J. (1985). Teacher clarity and its relationship to student achievement and satisfaction. *American Educational Research Journal, 22,* 87–99.

Horn, L. (1998). Stopouts or stayouts? Undergraduates who leave college in their first year (NCES No. 1999–087). Berkeley, CA: MPR Associates.

Howard, A. (1986). College experiences and managerial performance. *Journal of Applied Psychology Monographs, 71*(3), 530–552.

Hu, S., and Kuh, G. (2002). Being (dis)engaged in educationally purposeful activities: The influences of student and institutional characteristics. *Research in Higher Education, 43*(5), 555–575.

Hu, S., and Kuh, G. (2003a). Diversity experiences and college student learning and personal development. *Journal of College Student Development, 44*(3), 320–334.

Hu, S., and Kuh, G. (2003b). Maximizing what students get out of college: Testing a learning productivity model. *Journal of College Student Development, 44*(2), 185–203.

Hubbell, L., and Rush, S. (1991). A double-edged sword: Assessing the impact of tuition discounting. *Business Officer, 25*(6), 25–29.

Immerwahr, J., and Harvey, J. (1995, May 12). What the public thinks of college. *Chronicle of Higher Education, 41*(35), B1.

Inkelas, K., and Weisman, J. (2003). Different by design: An examination of student outcomes among participants in three types of living-learning programs. *Journal of College Student Development, 44*(3), 335–368.

Inman, P., and Pascarella, E. (1998). The impact of college residence on the development of critical thinking skills in college freshmen. *Journal of College Student Development, 39*(6), 557–568.

Ishitani, T., and DesJardins, S. (2002). A longitudinal investigation of dropout from college in the United States. *Journal of College Student Retention, 4*(2), 173–201.

Jacob, P. (1957). *Changing values in college: An exploratory study of the impact of college teaching.* New York: Harper & Row.

Johnson, D., Johnson, R., and Smith, K. (1998a). *Active learning: Cooperation in the college classroom* (2nd ed.). Edina, MN: Interaction Book Company.

Johnson, D., Johnson, R., and Smith, K. (1998b). Cooperative learning returns to college. *Change, 30*(4), 26–35.

Johnstone, K., Ashbaugh, H., and Warfield, T. (2002). Effects of repeated practice and contextual-writing experiences on college students' writing skills. *Journal of Educational Psychology, 94*(2), 305–315.

Kane, T. J. (1999). *The price of admission: Rethinking how Americans pay for college.* Washington, DC: Brookings Institution Press.

Kaufman, R., and Woglom, G. (2005). Financial changes and optimal spending rates of top liberal arts colleges, 1996–2001. *Review of Higher Education, 28*(3), 339–368.

Kimball, B. (1986). *Orators and philosophers: A history of the idea of liberal education.* New York: Teachers College Press.

Koblik, S. (2000). Foreword. In S. Koblik and S. Graubard (Eds.), *Distinctively American: The residential liberal arts colleges* (pp. xv–xvi). New Brunswick, NJ: Transaction Publishers.

Koblik, S., and Graubard, S. (Eds.). (2000). *Distinctively American: The residential liberal arts colleges.* New Brunswick, NJ: Transaction Publishers.

Kuh, G. (1993). In their own words: What students learn outside the classroom. *American Educational Research Journal, 30,* 277–304.

Kuh, G., and Hu, S. (1999, November). *Is more better? Student-faculty interaction revisited.* Paper presented at the annual meeting of the Association for the Study of Higher Education, San Antonio, TX.

Kuh, G., and Hu, S. (2001). Learning productivity at research universities. *Journal of Higher Education, 72*(1), 1–28.

Kuh, G., Pace, C., and Vesper, N. (1997). The development of process indicators to estimate student gains associated with good practices in undergraduate education. *Research in Higher Education, 38*(4), 435–454.

Kuh, G., and Pascarella, E. (2004). What does institutional selectivity tell us about educational quality? *Change, 36,* 52–58.

Kuh, G., Schuh, J., Whitt, E., and Associates. (1991). *Involving colleges.* San Francisco: Jossey-Bass.

Kuh, G., and others. (2005). *Student success in college.* San Francisco: Jossey-Bass.

Labaree, D. (1990). From comprehensive high school to community college: Politics, markets, and the evolution of educational opportunity. *Research in Sociology of Education and Socialization, 9,* 203–240.

Labaree, D. (2004). *The trouble with ed schools.* New Haven: Yale University Press.

Lagemann, E. (2003). The challenge of liberal education: Past, present, and future. *Liberal Education, 89*(2), 6–13.

Lang, E. (2000). Distinctively American: The liberal arts college. In S. Koblik and S. Graubard (Eds.), *Distinctively American: The residential liberal arts colleges* (pp. 133–150). New Brunswick, NJ: Transaction Publishers.

Lattuca, L., and Stark, J. (2001). Liberal studies and professional specialization. *AAC&U Peer Review, 3*(2), 4–8.

Leslie, D. (2002). Resolving the dispute: Teaching is academe's core value. *Journal of Higher Education, 73*(1), 49–73.

Ludlow, L. (1996). Instructor evaluation ratings: A longitudinal analysis. *Journal of Personnel Evaluation in Education, 10*(1), 83–92.

MacTaggart, T. (1993). The new vocationalism: Peril and promise. *Trusteeship, 1*(6), 6–9.

Marshall, G. (2003, September 12). A liberal education is not a luxury. *Chronicle of Higher Education,* B16.

McCormick, A. (1997). *Transfer behavior among beginning postsecondary students: 1989–94.* Washington, DC: National Center for Education Statistics.

McNeel, S. (1994). College teaching and student moral development. In J.R.D. Narvaez (Ed.), *Moral development in the professions: Psychology and applied ethics* (pp. 26–47). Hillsdale, NJ: Erlbaum.

McPherson, M. (1998). The economic value of a liberal arts education. *About Campus, 3*(4), 13–17.

McPherson, M., and Shapiro, M. (2000). Economic challenges for liberal arts colleges. In S. G. Koblik and S. R. Graubard (Eds.), *Distinctively American: The residential liberal arts colleges* (pp. 46–75). New Brunswick, NJ: Transaction Publishers.

Miles, S. (1986). *The vocational–liberal arts controversy: Looking backwards.* Sugar Grove, IL: Waubonsee Community College. (ED 292 496)

Mohrman, K. (1999). What really matters in the liberal arts. *Trusteeship, 7*(4), 8–12.

Monks, J. (2000). The returns to individual and college characteristics: Evidence from the National Longitudinal Survey of Youth. *Economics of Education Review, 19*(3), 279–289.

National Association of State Universities and Land-Grant Colleges. (1997). *Returning to our roots: The student experience.* Washington, DC: National Association of State Universities and Land-Grant Colleges.

National Center for Education Statistics. (2003). *Digest of education statistics and tables and figures,* Table 349. Retrieved April 19, 2005, from http://nces.ed.gov/programs/digest/d03/tables/dt349.asp.

National Survey of Student Engagement. (2004). *Student engagement: Pathways to collegiate success. 2004 Annual Survey Results.* Retrieved April 19, 2005, from http://www.indiana.edu/~nsse/html/annual_reports.htm.

Neely, P. (2000). The threat to liberal arts colleges. In S. Koblik and S. R. Graubard (Eds.), *Distinctively American: The residential liberal arts colleges* (pp. 27–45). New Brunswick, NJ: Transaction Publishers.

Newman, J. H. (1853/1996). *The idea of a university.* New Haven, CT: Yale University Press.

Nussbaum, M. (1997). *Cultivating humanity: A classical defense of reform in liberal education.* Cambridge, MA: Harvard University Press.

O'Brien, W. (1991). In quest of virtue: Liberal education and the ethics crisis. *Scholar and Educator, 15*(1–2), 22–30.

Pace, C. (1974). *The demise of diversity? A comparative profile of eight types of institutions.* Berkeley, CA: Carnegie Commission on Higher Education.

Pace, C. (1990). *The undergraduates.* Los Angeles: UCLA Center for the Study of Evaluation.

Pace, C. (1997, November). *Connecting institutional types to student outcomes.* Paper presented at the Association for the Study of Higher Education, Albuquerque, NM.

Pace, C., and Connolly, M. (2000). Where are the liberal arts? *Research in Higher Education, 41*(1), 53–65.

Pascarella, E. (2001). Using student self-reported gains to estimate college impact: A cautionary tale. *Journal of College Student Development, 42*(5), 488–492.

Pascarella, E., and Terenzini, P. (1991). *How college affects students.* San Francisco: Jossey-Bass.

Pascarella, E., and Terenzini, P. (1998). Studying college students in the 21st century: Meeting new challenges. *Review of Higher Education, 21*(2), 151–165.

Pascarella, E., and Terenzini, P. (2005). *How college affects students: Vol. 2. A third decade of research.* San Francisco: Jossey-Bass.

Pascarella, E., Wolniak, G., and Pierson, C. (2003). Explaining student growth in college when you don't think you are. *Journal of College Student Development, 44*(1), 122–125.

Pascarella, E., and others. (1996a). Effects of teacher organization/preparation and teacher skill/clarity on general cognitive skills in college. *Journal of College Student Development, 37*(1), 7–19.

Pascarella, E., and others. (1996b). Influences on students' openness to diversity and challenge in the first year of college. *Journal of Higher Education, 67,* 174–195.

Pascarella, E., and others. (1998). Does work inhibit cognitive development during college? *Educational Evaluation and Policy Analysis, 20*(2), 75–93.

Paulsen, M., and Smart, J. (Eds.). (2001). *The finance of higher education: Theory, research, policy, and practice.* New York: Agathon Press.

Pierson, C., Wolniak, G., Pascarella, E., and Flowers, L. (2003). Impacts of two-year and four-year college attendance on learning orientations. *Review of Higher Education, 26*(3), 299–321.

Pike, G., Kuh, G., and Gonyea, R. (2003). The relationship between institutional mission and students' involvement and educational outcomes. *Research in Higher Education, 44*(2), 241–261.

Pratt, L. (2003). Will budget troubles restructure higher education? *Academe, 89*(1), 32–37.

Qin, Z., Johnson, D., and Johnson, R. (1995). Cooperative versus competitive efforts and problem solving. *Review of Educational Research, 65,* 129–143.

Rosenfield, L. (1985). Civic virtue and the university of the future. *Association for Communication Administration Bulletin, 51,* 54–56.

Rothblatt, S. (2003). *The living arts: Comparative and historical reflections on liberal education. The academy in transition.* Washington, DC: Association of American Colleges and Universities.

Rudolph, F. (1990). *The American college and university: A history.* Athens: University of Georgia Press.

Schneider, C., and Shoenberg, R. (1998). *Contemporary understandings of liberal education: The academy in transition.* Washington, DC: Association of American Colleges and Universities.

Schwerin, U. (1983). Technical-career education must include liberal learning. *Improving College and University Teaching, 31*(4), 169–171.

Scott, B. (1992). The "new practicality" revisited: Changes in the American college curriculum. *Journal of Education, 174*(1), 87–103.

Seery, J. E. (2002). *America goes to college: Political theory for the liberal arts.* Albany: State University of New York Press.

Shea, C. (1993). Idealism and economic pragmatism mix in debate over value of liberal arts. *Chronicle of Higher Education, 39*(25), A16.

Smart, J. (1997). Academic subenvironments and differential patterns of self-perceived growth during college: A test of Holland's theory. *Journal of College Student Development, 38*(1), 68–77.

Spaeth, R. (1986). Ideas have consequences—or do they? *College Teaching, 43*(1), 17–19.

Springer, L., and others. (1996). Attitudes toward campus diversity: Participation in a racial or cultural awareness workshop. *Review of Higher Education, 20*(1), 53–68.

Stark, J. (1987). Liberal education and professional programs: Conflict, coexistence, or compatibility? *New Directions for Higher Education, 15*(1), 91–102.

Stratton, C. (1990). *The effects of a liberal arts college education on the values and attitudes of students.* Unpublished doctoral dissertation, University of Alabama, Tuscaloosa.

Terenzini, P., and others. (1994). *The multiple influences on students' critical thinking skills.* Paper presented at the annual meeting of the Association for the Study of Higher Education, Orlando, FL.

Terenzini, P., and others. (2001). Collaborative learning vs. lecture/discussion: Students' reported learning gains. *Journal of Engineering Education, 90,* 123–130.

Thelin, J. (2004). *A history of American higher education.* Baltimore: Johns Hopkins University Press.

Tinto, V., and Goodsell, A. (1994). Freshman interest groups and the first-year experience: Constructing student communities in a large university. *Journal of the Freshman Year Experience, 6,* 7–27.

Tsapogas, J., Cahalan, M., and Stowe, P. (1994). *Academic institutional characteristics and the educational labor market outcomes of recent college graduates: An exploratory analysis.* Paper presented at the annual meeting of the Association for Institutional Research, New Orleans, LA.

Umbach, P., and Kuh, G. (forthcoming). Student experiences with diversity at liberal arts colleges: Another claim for distinctiveness. *Journal of Higher Education.*

Upcraft, M. L., Gardner, J., and Associates (1989). *The freshman year experience: Helping students survive and succeed in college.* San Francisco: Jossey-Bass.

Useem, M. (1989). *Liberal education and the corporation: The hiring and advancement of college graduates.* Hawthorne, NY: Aldine de Gruyter.

Volkwein, J., and Carbone, D. (1994). The impact of department research and teaching climate on undergraduate growth and satisfaction. *Journal of Higher Education, 65*(2), 147–167.

Wachtel, H. (1998). Student evaluation of college teaching effectiveness: A brief review. *Assessment and Evaluation in Higher Education, 23*(2), 191–211.

Waterman, A. (Ed.). (1997). *Service-learning: Applications from the research.* Mahwah, NJ: Erlbaum.

Watson, L., and Kuh, G. (1996). The influence of dominant race environments on students involvement, perceptions, and educational gains: A look at historically black and predominantly white liberal arts institutions. *Journal of College Student Development, 37*(4), 415–424.

Whitmire, E., and Lawrence, J. (1996, November). *Undergraduate students' development of critical thinking skills: An institutional and disciplinary analysis and comparison with academic library use and other measures.* Paper presented at the annual meeting of the Association for the Study of Higher Education, Memphis, TN.

Whitt, E., and others. (1999). Interactions with peers and objective and self-reported cognitive outcomes across three years of college. *Journal of College Student Development, 40*(1), 61–78.

Whitt, E., and others. (2001). Influences on students' openness to diversity and challenge in the second and third years of college. *Journal of Higher Education, 72*(2), 172–204.

Wilkinson, R. (1964). *Gentlemanly power: British leadership and the public school tradition.* London: Oxford University Press.

Wingspread Group on Higher Education. (1993). *An American imperative: Higher expectations for higher education.* Racine, WI: Johnson Foundation.

Winter, D., McClelland, D., and Stewart, A. (1981). *A new case for the liberal arts.* San Francisco: Jossey-Bass.

Wolniak, G., Pierson, C., and Pascarella, E. (2001). Effects of intercollegiate athletic participation on male orientations toward learning. *Journal of College Student Development, 42*(6), 604–623.

Wood, A., and Murray, H. (1999, April). *Effects of teacher enthusiasm on student attention, motivation, and memory encoding.* Paper presented at the annual meeting of the American Educational Research Association, Montreal, QC.

Zlotkowski, E. (Ed.). (2002). *Service-learning and the first-year experience: Preparing students for personal success and civic responsibility.* Columbia, SC: National Resource Center for the First-Year Experience and Students in Transition.

Name Index

A

Abrami, P., 32
Adelman, C., 20
Ahson, N., 20
Aleman, A.M.M., 4
Alwin, D., 36, 46
Anaya, G., 32
Arnold, J., 32
Ashbaugh, H., 32
Astin, A., 4, 10, 11, 13, 20, 23, 31, 32, 54, 59, 89
Atkinson, D., 10, 12

B

Barker, C., 9, 10
Beck, R., 98
Bellas, M., 21, 22
Bird, C., 12
Blaich, C., 59, 105
Boehner, J., 10
Bok, D., 28
Bonvillian, G., 8, 11
Bost, A., 59
Bowen, H., 92
Bowen, W., 28
Bray, G., 32, 93
Breneman, D., 2, 4, 5, 6, 11
Brint, S., 6, 7, 8
Brown, F., 19

C

Cabrera, A., 32
Cahalan, M., 21

Carbone, D., 33
Carini, R., 33
Carnevale, A., 11
Cartwright, C., 20
Cejda, B., 105
Chan, E., 59
Chickering, A., 1, 8, 31, 32, 54, 88, 90
Clark, B., 54
Connolly, M., 2, 14, 16
Conrad, C., 3, 18
Cronon, W., 1
Cruce, T., 93
Cruickshank, D., 32

D

d'Appollonia, S., 32
Davis, T., 31, 32, 33
Delucchi, M., 5
DesJardins, S., 20
Douzenis, C., 33
Duemer, L., 105
Durden, W., 2, 8, 11, 12

E

Ethington, C., 32

F

Feldman, K., 31
Finkelstein, M., 14
Fitzgerald, R., 21, 22
Flowers, L., 46
Freedman, J., 3, 6, 11

Subject Index

A
Appalachian College Association
(ACA) study
  data from, 71–73
  description of, 26–30

C
Carnegie classification, 4–5, 14, 21, 26
Challenges to liberal arts colleges, 6–12
Citizenship, responsible
  as educational goal, 1, 3
  as long-term effect, 72, 73, 95
  study results on, 74, 76, 79, 81
  in younger alumni, 83, 85, 100
College Student Experiences Questionnaire
  (CSEQ), 14, 17, 27, 108, 110, 111
Collegiate Assessment of Academic
  Proficiency (CAAP) tests, 45, 47,
  114–115
Conclusions, monograph, 101–103.
  See also Summary of findings
Conditional effects
  defined, 33
  good practices and, 39
  importance of, 103
  long-term effects as, 82–85, 99
  personal development and, 57–58
  summary of findings on, xi, 98–100

D
Datasets, description of, vii, 26–28
Denominational liberal arts colleges,
  defined, 4

Diversity, openness to
  defined, 115–116
  past research on, 18–19
  study results on, 51-52, 92

E
Earnings of graduates
  as long-term effect, 72
  past research on, 21–22
  study results on, 75, 77, 83, 84

F
Faculty
  quality of teaching by, 32, 35, 39,
    42, 43
  student-faculty contact, 31, 32, 34, 39,
    41, 43
Financial resources of colleges, 11, 102–103
First-year impact, 57, 90, 92

G
G. I. Bill, 8
General liberal arts colleges
  defined, 4
  future earnings and, 22
  learning productivity and, 15
Good practices
  analysis of, 1
  conditional effects on, 39
  defined, 31–32
  direct effects on, 36, 37–39
  major findings on, viii, 87–90
  study results on, 33–37

timing of effects on, 39–44
total effects on, 36, 37
Graduate degree attainment
as labor market outcome, 74, 76
as long-term effect, 71, 95
study results on, 82, 83, 95

H

Health-related behaviors
as long-term effect, 71, 73
study results on, 80–81
History of liberal arts colleges, 1, 3–4, 6–12

I

Industrial Revolution, 7
Institutional size, 11, 88–89
Institutional types
descriptions of, 4–6, 93–94 future
earnings and, 21–22, 75, 77, 83, 84, 96
good practices and, 31–44, 87–90
student development and, 15–20, 45–58, 91–95
student engagement and, 14–15, 102
student persistence and, 20–21
Intellectual and personal development
analysis of, 1–2
data on, 45–50
first-year impact on, 57, 92
liberal arts emphasis and, 59–70
measures of, 45, 47
past research on, 12–13, 15–20
study results on, 50–58
summary of findings on, viii–x, 91–95

L

Labor market outcomes
as long-term effect, 71, 72
study results on, 74–75, 76–77
tuition increases and, 10
Liberal arts colleges
challenges facing, 6–12
conclusions on, 101–103

history of, 1, 3–4, 6–12
long-term effects of, 71–85
mission of, 3–4, 11
student engagement at, 13–15, 88
types of, 4–6, 14–15, 102
Liberal arts education
goals of, 3–4, 9–12
summary on, 87–100
Liberal arts emphasis
analysis of, 2, 59–62
conditional effects of, 68–70
defined, 59–61
net effects of, 61, 62–66
student development and, 93–95
Liberal arts experiences (LAEXP)
conditional effects of, 68–70
defined, 60, 61
positive effects of, 66–68
student development and, 93–95
study results on, 62, 63–64
Literature review
general description of, 2–3
as study background, 3–22
summary of, 22–23
Long-term effects
analysis of, 2
conditional, 82–85, 99–100
data on, 71–73
past research on, 20–22
study results on, 74–85
summary of findings on, x, 95–98

M

Mathematics skills, 47, 48, 53, 91, 114
Moral reasoning, 19–20

N

National Study of Student Learning
(NSSL) database
description of, 26–30
good practices data from, 31–33
student development data from, 45–50, 59–62
National Study of Student Engagement
(NSSE), 16, 102

About the Authors

Ernest T. Pascarella is the Mary Louise Petersen Chair in Higher Education at The University of Iowa. His research focuses on the impact of college on students. He has received the research awards of the Association for Institutional Research, the Association for the Study of Higher Education, Division J of the American Educational Research Association, the American College Personnel Association, the National Association of Student Personnel Administrators, and the International Reading Association. In 1990, he was president of the Association for the Study of Higher Education and in 2003 received that organization's Howard R. Bowen Distinguished Career Award.

Gregory C. Wolniak is a postdoctoral research scholar in the Division of Educational Policy and Leadership Studies at The University of Iowa. A recent graduate of Iowa's Social Foundations of Education doctoral program, his research focuses on the career, labor market, and socioeconomic outcomes of education. For his doctoral dissertation, he tested a causal model of job satisfaction by focusing on college majors and major-job field congruence. A version of this work will appear in the *Journal of Vocational Behavior;* his other publications have appeared in *Journal of College Student Development, Journal of Higher Education, Research in Higher Education,* and *Electronic Journal of Sociology.*

Tricia A. Seifert is a doctoral student in the Student Affairs Administration and Research program at The University of Iowa. She recently received an ACPA Commission IX grant for a mixed methods study investigating the role of institutional type in students' experiences of good practices in undergraduate education. She has presented her research at ASHE, ACPA, and NASPA. She also serves as a research assistant for the National Study of Liberal Arts Education sponsored by the Center of Inquiry in the Liberal Arts at Wabash College. Her research interests include the cognitive, psychosocial, and socioeconomic impact of postsecondary educational attainment, experiences of faculty, and organizational leadership.

Ty M. Cruce is a research associate with the Indiana University Center for Postsecondary Research, where he serves as project manager of the Beginning College Survey of Student Engagement and as a research analyst for the National Survey of Student Engagement. He received his doctorate in higher education at The University of Iowa. His current research focuses on educational transitions and the impact of student engagement on college outcomes.

Charles F. Blaich currently serves as director of inquiries at the Center of Inquiry in the Liberal Arts. Before his work at the center, Blaich's research focused on animal communication in mallard ducks and zebra finches. He received his Ph.D. in psychology from the University of Connecticut in 1986, taught at Eastern Illinois University from 1987–1991, and joined the psychology department at Wabash College in 1991.

About the ASHE Higher Education Reports Series

Since 1983, the ASHE (formerly ASHE-ERIC) Higher Education Report Series has been providing researchers, scholars, and practitioners with timely and substantive information on the critical issues facing higher education. Each monograph presents a definitive analysis of a higher education problem or issue, based on a thorough synthesis of significant literature and institutional experiences. Topics range from planning to diversity and multiculturalism, to performance indicators, to curricular innovations. The mission of the Series is to link the best of higher education research and practice to inform decision making and policy. The reports connect conventional wisdom with research and are designed to help busy individuals keep up with the higher education literature. Authors are scholars and practitioners in the academic community. Each report includes an executive summary, review of the pertinent literature, descriptions of effective educational practices, and a summary of key issues to keep in mind to improve educational policies and practice.

The Series is one of the most peer reviewed in higher education. A National Advisory Board made up of ASHE members reviews proposals. A National Review Board of ASHE scholars and practitioners reviews completed manuscripts. Six monographs are published each year and they are approximately 120 pages in length. The reports are widely disseminated through Jossey-Bass and John Wiley & Sons, and they are available online to subscribing institutions through Wiley InterScience (http://www.interscience.wiley.com).

Call for Proposals

The ASHE Higher Education Report Series is actively looking for proposals. We encourage you to contact one of the editors, Dr. Kelly Ward (kaward@wsu.edu) or Dr. Lisa Wolf-Wendel (lwolf@ku.edu), with your ideas.

Recent Titles

2. Faculty Compensation Systems: Impact on the Quality of Higher Education
    Terry P. Sutton, Peter J. Bergerson
3. Socialization of Graduate and Professional Students in Higher Education:
    A Perilous Passage?
    John C. Weidman, Darla J. Twale, Elizabeth Leahy Stein
4. Understanding and Facilitating Organizational Change in the 21st Century: Recent
    Research and Conceptualizations
    Adrianna J. Kezar
5. Cost Containment in Higher Education: Issues and Recommendations
    Walter A. Brown, Cayo Gamber
6. Facilitating Students' Collaborative Writing
    Bruce W. Speck

Liberal Arts Colleges and Liberal Arts Education

Back Issue/Subscription Order Form

Copy or detach and send to:

Jossey-Bass, A Wiley Imprint, 989 Market Street, San Francisco CA 94103-1741

Call or fax toll-free: Phone 888-378-2537 6:30AM – 3PM PST; Fax 888-481-2665

Back Issues: Please send me the following issues at $24 each

(Important: please include series abbreviation and issue number. For example ASHE 28:1)

_____

_____

_____

$ _____   Total for single issues

$ _____   SHIPPING CHARGES: SURFACE   Domestic Canadian
                                    First Item $5.00 $6.00
                                    Each Add'l Item $3.00 $1.50
                 For next-day and second-day delivery rates, call the number listed above

Subscriptions   Please ❑ start ❑ renew my subscription to *ASHE Higher Education Reports* for the year 2_____at the following rate:

U.S.	❑ Individual $165	❑ Institutional $175
Canada	❑ Individual $165	❑ Institutional $235
All Others	❑ Individual $213	❑ Institutional $286

❑ Online subscriptions available too!

**For more information about online subscriptions visit
www.interscience.wiley.com**

$ _____   Total single issues and subscriptions (Add appropriate sales tax for your state for single issue orders. No sales tax for U.S. subscriptions. Canadian residents, add GST for subscriptions and single issues.)

❑Payment enclosed (U.S. check or money order only)

❑VISA ❑ MC ❑ AmEx ❑ #_____ Exp. Date _____

Signature _____ Day Phone _____

❑ Bill Me (U.S. institutional orders only. Purchase order required.)

Purchase order # _____
                 Federal Tax ID13559302   GST 89102 8052

Name _____

Address _____

_____

Phone _____ E-mail _____

For more information about Jossey-Bass, visit our Web site at **www.josseybass.com**

Errata

The authors of the previous issue of the ASHE Higher Education report were not credited appropriately. *The Challenge of Diversity: Involvement or Alienation in the Academy?* (vol. 31, no. 1) was written by Daryl G. Smith in 1989, and it was reissued this year. Only the monograph's new introduction was co-authored by Daryl G. Smith and Lisa E. Wolf-Wendel. The entire volume should not have been attributed to both Smith and Wolf-Wendel, and the publisher regrets the error.